From Dreams to
DESTINY

A practical guide to Achieving you Aspirations

Claudia Vazquez

From Dreams to
DESTINY

©Copyright 2024, Claudia Vazquez
All rights reserved.

All rights reserved. No portion of this book may be reproduced by mechanical, photographic or electronic process, nor may it be stored in a retrieval system, transmitted in any form or otherwise be copied for public use or private use without written permission of the copyright owner.

Published by Fig Factor Media, LLC | www.figfactormedia.com

Cover Design by Juan Pablo Ruiz
Layout by LDG Juan Manuel Serna Rosales

Printed in the United States of America

ISBN: 978-1-961600-17-1
Library of Congress Control Number: 2024913323

This book is dedicated to the cherished constellation of individuals in my life: my husband of three decades, Paco, whose unwavering support and boundless love provide me with stability and objective perspective; our three sons, Francisco Axel, Enzo Alberto, and Ian Adonay, who have illuminated my existence, made me feel what unconditional love is, and enabled me to connect with my authentic self. To my tribe—my mother, sister and nephew, my extended family, intimate friends, and the advocates and mentors who have unwaveringly supported me—your presence in my life has shaped me into the person I am today.

TABLE OF CONTENTS

Acknowledgements 5

Introduction 6

How to Use This Book 9

    CHAPTER 1: DARE TO DREAM 11

    CHAPTER 2: MAKE A PLAN 29

    CHAPTER 3: STICK TO THE PLAN 49

    CHAPTER 4: BE GRATEFUL 69

    CHAPTER 5: LIFT OTHERS 83

    CHAPTER 6: FEEL GOOD 99

    CHAPTER 7: FIND YOUR TRIBE 113

    CHAPTER 8: LET GO 129

Conclusion: Turning Dreams into Destiny 145

About the Author 148

ACKNOWLEDGMENTS

Gratitude, the act of being thankful and acknowledging others, lies at the core of the success journey. In the book *Today's Inspired Latina, Volume 5*, where I had the privilege of sharing my story, I began with the quote, "Surround yourself with those who believe in the beauty of your dreams." This book has been a passion project for me over the past three decades, and its realization wouldn't have been possible without the unwavering support of Jacqueline Camacho Ruiz. Her boundless energy, passion, and vision spurred me on to bring this project to fruition. I am deeply indebted to my family, friends, mentors and advocates who have supported me, seeing potential in me that I may not have seen in myself. I'm also grateful to those who have extended their generosity and support to me and my family, going above and beyond to demonstrate their commitment to our family success. This book is the result of a collective effort of trust, encouragement, and pure love. Gracias!

INTRODUCTION

In 2007, upon returning from Washington, D.C., after receiving the Hispanic Association of Corporate Responsibility (HACR) Young Hispanic Corporate Achievers™ (YHCA) Award, I was approached by our human resources department to reflect on my journey and share my story with minority high school students visiting our office for a tour. The students had been nominated by their school district for showing potential and interest in going to college. They were eager to learn about job shadowing and to explore the insurance sector as a potential career path. I was honored to be designated as the keynote speaker for this occasion, marking my first experience addressing an audience of over fifty students. Since then, I've had the opportunity to share my narrative at prestigious institutions, like Princeton University and Yale University, as well as at underprivileged, predominantly minority middle schools in New Jersey, Texas, and Florida through Hispanics Inspiring Student's Performance and Achievement (HISPA), a 501(c)3 nonprofit dedicated to mobilizing Hispanic professionals to serve as role models for youth.

The YHCA is a program that serves as a platform to highlight the remarkable accomplishments of young Hispanic professionals in corporate America, aiming to advance the mission of enhancing Hispanic representation on corporate boards and in executive positions. I had the privilege of being part of the inaugural class, alongside esteemed Latinos from various industries across the United States.

Reflecting on my personal journey as a middle class girl in Mexico, and as a daughter of divorced parents, who had to start working at the age of fifteen to help with some of her own expenses and then later moving to the United States and becoming an English-as-a-second-language student, navigating the challenges of being a first-generation college attendee, living in a car garage converted into a studio, and seizing opportunities as a Latina woman in a Fortune 500 company, I sought to underscore the message that with a dream, a plan, perseverance, resilience, and gratitude, all aspirations are within reach.

I strived to connect with these students and present the material in a digestible manner, with the hope of inspiring them to take control of their lives and futures. For many young individuals without household role models or as first-generation college-goers, the path forward may seem uncertain or unattainable. However, it's important to recognize that such obstacles can be overcome.

To aid in this personal journey, I developed the Five Steps to Success, a straightforward framework that anyone can follow. While I have since refined it and added supplementary steps, the core principles remain unchanged. It's essential for each of us to define our aspirations clearly and pursue them with determination, resilience, and adaptability.

My purpose is to motivate individuals to take action in their lives, regardless of their current circumstances. Whether at a crossroads or seeking a fresh start, it's never too late to reinvent oneself or chart a new course.

Success demands grit, a balance between work and life, and unwavering determination. Progress may not always follow a linear path, but it requires continuous movement and growth. As chief executive officers (CEOs) of our own careers, we must not allow things to happen to us; rather, we should actively shape our destinies and strive to make things happen for us.

Arguably the most challenging aspect lies in taking that initial step, particularly when you're sincerely pursuing your dreams. At times, even our closest friends and loved ones may harbor reservations, seeking to shield us from perceived risks by nudging us toward safer paths or careers. While this inclination is natural, it falls upon each one of us to assertively advocate for ourselves and our aspirations, persistently maintaining our course. Time flies, and rather than spending energy worrying over potential setbacks, let's redirect our focus, efforts, and strategies toward actualizing our dream.

In my keynote address, "Mapping Your Career to Achieve Your Dreams," delivered virtually in March of 2018 to a global audience, I began with a simple yet crucial task—identify your passion. I emphasized to the participants that this process necessitates introspection and self-awareness, as oftentimes we may have forgotten the aspirations we held dear in our youth. Reconnecting with our childhood essence is the catalyst for igniting the spark of life within us! Certain skills are innate to us, and they typically align with activities that bring us joy because they come naturally. I'm thrilled that you've chosen to read this book, and I encourage you to breeze through its chapters with one objective in mind: rediscovering yourself and being true to your authentic dreams, while finding the power within you to take action and make it a reality!

HOW TO USE THIS BOOK

This book will include personal stories that will serve as personal life examples of the concepts discussed. It will also include definitions, practical guides on the concepts revealed, and, in some cases, thought-provoking questions so you can begin to connect with your highest self and manifest your life purpose. This book is intended and would work exponentially to your advantage if paired with the From Dreams to Destiny Diary. The meticulously designed diary provides a structured framework to help readers implement the principles and strategies outlined in the book, empowering them to turn their dreams into reality. Featuring thought-provoking prompts, insightful exercises, and guided reflections, the diary serves as a personal coach, guiding readers through their journey of self-discovery and goal attainment. In addition, my philosophy lies around the ability to have fun with others while learning, as a result I created From Dreams to Destiny deck of cards that can be used to reinforce the topics mentioned in the book and diary.

FROM DREAMS TO DESTINY

Chapter 1

DARE TO DREAM

Breaking Boundaries: Dare to Dream Beyond Limits

It all begins in childhood, where our imagination runs wild, and we envision ourselves as someone special. For me, these childhood fantasies often revolved around two main roles and two defining traits. I would either play the role of the "pregnant teacher," sporting a pillow beneath my shirt to mimic a late-stage pregnancy, or the "successful executive at the United Nations," sitting behind a desk, issuing orders with authority. These memories hold a special place in my heart.

My early years in Guadalajara, Jalisco, Mexico, were shaped by the unique living arrangement in a two-apartment building, with my mother and me occupying one unit, while my grandmother and cousin resided in the other. The two apartments were interconnected, fostering a sense of unity and shared space. My grandmother, who was also my caregiver, hosted domestic and international university students and bank employees, turning our home into a hub of creativity and learning. Afternoons were filled with macramé, painting, sewing, and even yoga sessions, providing a rich tapestry of experiences.

Despite being a middle-class family, my upbringing included certain luxuries, thanks to my mother's job in an American investment company. Early on, I was introduced to the joys of owning a stereo and a portable typewriter, sparking my imagination and creativity. Even simple items like wooden boxes became catalysts for elaborate living room plays, where I would entertain my cousins with imaginative scenarios.

Reflecting on those formative years, I realize the profound impact they had on shaping my dreams and aspirations. My mother's encouragement to dream big and push beyond my limits fueled my passion and creativity. As psychologists and development experts suggest, the first seven years of a child's life are crucial for laying the foundation for success, fostering trust, autonomy, and initiative.

CHAPTER 1: DARE TO DREAM

I encourage you to revisit your own childhood dreams and aspirations. **What did you dream of when playing with friends or doodling on paper?** These early inclinations often hold clues to our true passions and strengths. By connecting with our authentic selves and embracing our childhood dreams, we can find fulfillment and purpose in our journey.

BREAKING BOUNDARIES

Under the beautiful and bright blue Zipolite sky, nestled against its sandy shores in Oaxaca, Mexico, my journey of self-discovery unfolded. At twenty-two, while my husband was twenty-five and pursued his medical studies, we resided in this coastal haven. His commitment to serving the underserved population led us to immerse ourselves in the community, where I found my own path of service.

Accompanying my husband in his medical duties, I found myself aiding in various capacities, from administering immunizations to assisting in childbirth. These experiences ignited a realization within me—my purpose lay in serving others. Yet, the question lingered, how could I best fulfill this calling?

Initially treating our stay as a vacation, I soon felt a stirring within me, a desire for something more. Reflecting on my skills and experiences, I recognized the opportunity to bridge a gap in the community's needs. With my proficiency in English and a multicultural upbringing, I saw the potential to impart English language skills to the local children, fulfilling both a community need and a childhood dream of mine.

Launching English as a Second Language (ESL) classes, I found immediate interest from the village. With makeshift materials and a passion for teaching, I crafted lesson plans and managed classes effortlessly. The work not only brought joy and fulfillment but also honed my creativity, compassion, and resilience—reaffirming my dedication to serving others.

This journey led me to pursue formal certification as an ESL teacher, when we moved to Mexico City marking the beginning of a transformative chapter. Upon relocating to California a few years after, I continued my mission, balancing full-time work, volunteering, and furthering my college education. My time spent teaching ESL to Hispanic students at a local community center became cherished memories, fueling my determination to make a broader impact.

In 1996, the decision to settle permanently in Pasadena, California, marked a significant turning point in my life. The driving force behind this decision was multifaceted, with one primary goal in mind: to pursue and to complete my bachelor's degree, a dream long deferred due to financial constraints and frequent relocations.

Upon our arrival in Pasadena, I wasted no time in taking the necessary steps to realize this ambition. Visiting the nearest community college campus, I underwent a series of placement tests, only to discover that my English proficiency fell below expectations. Undeterred by this setback, I followed the counselor's advice and enrolled in multiple English classes, recognizing that clarity of purpose and a well-defined plan were essential prerequisites for success.

Over the subsequent six years, I embarked on a journey characterized by unwavering determination and tireless effort. Balancing full-time employment, the joys of impending motherhood, and the complexities of homeownership, I steadfastly pursued my academic goals while also embracing opportunities to serve others. Volunteering as an ESL teacher and citizenship instructor, I had the privilege of guiding dozens of Hispanic students through the process of obtaining U.S. citizenship—a deeply rewarding experience that underscored the profound impact of perseverance and dedication.

CHAPTER 1: DARE TO DREAM

Yet, amid the triumphs lay moments of self-doubt and uncertainty. Confronted with the complexities of economic theory, statistical analysis, and professional setbacks, I grappled with feelings of inadequacy and questioned my capacity to excel in academia and the corporate world alike. However, rather than succumbing to despair or resignation, I chose to confront these challenges head-on, drawing upon a reservoir of resilience and unwavering resolve.

At the age of thirty, a pivotal milestone marked the culmination of my academic journey: the birth of our first child coincided with my graduation with a degree in psychology—a profound testament to the power of perseverance and the fulfillment of a generational aspiration.

Lifted by this achievement, I continued to chart a course marked by relentless pursuit of personal and professional growth. Completing a master's degree, assuming managerial responsibilities, and embracing opportunities to effect positive change within my community and workplace, I found fulfillment in aligning my passion with purpose.

As I reflect on the milestones achieved and the challenges overcome, I am reminded of the invaluable support and encouragement extended by my husband, family, friends, mentors, and colleagues. Indeed, success is not a solitary endeavor but a collaborative effort, grounded in the collective belief in the boundless potential of the human spirit.

In essence, my journey underscores the profound truth that with grit, resilience, and unwavering determination, the attainment of one's dreams is not merely possible—it is inevitable.

DREAMING BEYOND LIMITS

As I embraced the role of motherhood, and sincere gratitude for the blessing of giving birth to three boys, a newfound avenue for contribution unfolded before me: volunteering at my children's school. Eager to make a meaningful impact, I immersed myself in every opportunity that arose. It began with reading to the class, a simple yet gratifying experience that ignited a passion for educational enrichment.

Soon, I found myself delving deeper, crafting tailored lesson plans suited to the diverse age groups within the school. These plans weren't just about imparting knowledge; they were about nurturing self-discovery and building confidence in each child. From interactive activities to engaging discussions, I sought to create a learning environment that was both stimulating and empowering.

The next evolution in my journey came with planned visits to the school, where I had the opportunity to deliver hands-on activities directly to the students. These activities weren't just educational; they were transformative experiences designed to ignite curiosity and to foster a love for learning. Over time, I developed and delivered over forty workshops for children, each one focused on unlocking their potential and unleashing their inner strengths.

Why did I incorporate games and physical activities into every workshop? Because I understood that most children are kinesthetic learners, meaning they learn best through hands-on experiences. For them, active participation is key to understanding and retaining information. Whether it was building pinwheels to learn about wind energy or engaging in role-playing exercises, I strived to create immersive learning experiences that resonated with each child's unique learning style.

But my journey didn't stop at the classroom door. Recognizing the potential to reach beyond the confines of the school, I embarked on a mission to expand my impact.

CHAPTER 1: DARE TO DREAM

In 2016, drawing inspiration from my own experiences and the overarching themes of my story, I conceptualized and launched Univerbond Camp—a transformative program dedicated to children aged eight to twelve.

Modeled after the traditional summer camp format, Univerbond Camp offered a dynamic blend of education and adventure. With themed "cabins" and exciting activities like fishing, hiking, and arrow throwing, the camp aimed to instill valuable life skills while fostering a sense of camaraderie and teamwork among participants.

The success of Univerbond Camp propelled me further on my journey. Armed with invaluable experience and a passion for empowering young minds, I began facilitating lessons with various Girl Scout troops in the area. It was a dream come true, and it marked the first foundational block in my entrepreneurial journey—an adventure filled with boundless possibilities and endless opportunities for growth and impact.

In 2020, fueled by a desire to catalyze greater change, I embarked on a personal journey that would reshape the landscape of professional development. With a vision to foster inclusivity in the workplace, I founded **elevink**, LLC—a social impact company committed to empowering underrepresented talent and cultivating a more diverse and equitable workforce.

What began as a humble two-day boot camp swiftly evolved into a comprehensive talent development program. Rooted in the belief that everyone deserves access to opportunities for personal and professional growth, elevink's mission equips individuals with the skills and confidence needed to thrive in today's competitive job market.

Our program is designed to address the unique challenges faced by underrepresented groups, offering a holistic approach to skill-building and career advancement. From crafting personalized elevator pitches to navigating job descriptions with a critical eye, we guide participants through every step of the job search process.

But our impact extends far beyond mere job placement. At elevink, we understand that true success lies in empowering individuals to become agents of change in their own lives and communities. That's why our program includes workshops on communication style, resilience-building, and diversity and inclusion—ensuring that our graduates are not only prepared for success but also equipped to effect positive change in their workplaces and beyond.

With each cohort, we strive to create a supportive and inclusive learning environment where participants can connect, collaborate, and grow together. Our Monday night sessions provide a platform for meaningful discussions and networking opportunities, while our roster of subject matter experts offers valuable insights and guidance to help participants navigate their career journeys.

Despite the challenges posed by the pandemic, we remain steadfast in our commitment to accessibility and inclusivity. By offering our program virtually, we've been able to reach individuals from across the country, from bustling metropolises like New York and Chicago to quieter corners of Texas and New Jersey.

The impact of elevink is palpable, with each cohort leaving a lasting imprint on our community. Graduation ceremonies are not just celebrations of achievement but also poignant reminders of the transformative power of education and opportunity. And the results speak for themselves: nearly half of our graduates report securing promotions, new jobs, or making career changes within sixty days of completing the program.

As we look to the future, we're inspired by the stories of success and resilience that continue to emerge from our program. Through our monthly podcast, elevink Connect, we aim to spark new ideas and inspire professionals to take action for their own career success.

At elevink, our mission is clear: to empower individuals to reach their full potential and to create a more inclusive and equitable future for all. With each new cohort, we're one step closer to realizing that vision.

THE "HOW-TO"

Let's shift our focus from reminiscing about the unfolding of my childhood dreams to the core essence of this book—a deliberate emphasis on guidance and practicality. I firmly believe in tangible results and the pragmatic "how-to" aspect of achieving goals. Therefore, this book isn't merely a collection of personal anecdotes supported by facts or white papers. Instead, its purpose is to equip you with actionable steps to realize your aspirations.

Each chapter is meticulously structured to include a comprehensive guide tailored to your journey of self-discovery and accomplishment. The aim is to provide you with practical tools and strategies that you can implement immediately. Furthermore, by utilizing the accompanying diary, navigating through these steps becomes even more seamless and efficient.

The intention behind this approach is clear—to bridge the gap between inspiration and execution. It's not enough to dream; we must also have a roadmap to transform those dreams into reality. This book serves as your compass, offering practical insights and actionable advice to guide you along your path to success.

With a focus on practicality and results-driven strategies, you'll find that each chapter is designed to empower you with the knowledge and tools necessary to overcome obstacles and achieve your goals. By incorporating the guide and workbook into your journey, you'll not only streamline your efforts but also increase your chances of success.

So, let's embark on this transformative journey together, armed with the practical wisdom and guidance contained within these pages. By taking deliberate action and leveraging the tools provided, you'll be well-equipped to turn your aspirations into achievements.

The first step of this journey and the foundation of Dare to Dream is having a North Star. Having a North Star, a guiding principle or goal that directs one's actions and decisions, is essential for navigating life's journey with purpose and clarity. Just as ancient mariners relied on the North Star to guide their ships across vast oceans, having a personal North Star provides individuals with a constant beacon of light amid life's uncertainties.

One of the key benefits of having a North Star is that it provides a sense of direction and focus. In a world filled with distractions and competing priorities, knowing what truly matters to you can help you filter out the noise and stay aligned with your goals. Whether it's a long-term vision for your career, a commitment to personal growth, or a set of values that guide your decisions, your North Star serves as a compass, helping you stay on course even when the path ahead seems unclear.

Having a North Star also brings a sense of purpose and meaning to your life. When you have a clear understanding of what you're working towards, every action you take feels purposeful and intentional. This sense of purpose can be incredibly motivating, driving you to overcome obstacles and persevere in the face of challenges.

Moreover, a North Star can provide a source of resilience during difficult times. When you encounter setbacks or failures, having a guiding principle to fall back on can help you to stay grounded and focused on the bigger picture. Rather than getting lost in despair or self-doubt, you can draw strength from your North Star and use it as a source of inspiration to keep moving forward.

Furthermore, a North Star can serve as a source of alignment and coherence in your life. By defining your core values and priorities, you can ensure that your actions and decisions are in harmony with your true self. This alignment brings a sense of integrity and authenticity to your life, allowing you to live in accordance with your deepest beliefs and aspirations.

In addition, a North Star can foster a sense of connection and community. When you are clear about what you stand for and what you are working towards, you are more likely to attract like-minded individuals who share your values and goals. This sense of belonging can be incredibly empowering, as it allows you to surround yourself with people who support and inspire you on your journey.

Ultimately, having a North Star is not about reaching a specific destination or achieving a particular outcome. Instead, it's about embracing the journey and staying true to yourself along the way. Whether it's guiding you towards personal growth, professional success, or a deeper sense of fulfillment, your North Star is a constant reminder that the path you're on is uniquely yours—and that the possibilities are endless.

The second step of this journey and the foundation of Dare to Dream is to have clarity of the goals to be achieved. Having clarity of our desired destiny is crucial for achieving fulfillment and success in life. Just as a ship needs a clear destination to chart its course, knowing where we want to go provides us with direction, purpose, and motivation. Here are several reasons why having clarity of our desired destiny is important:

1. **Focus and Direction:** Clarity of our desired destiny

helps us to focus our energy and efforts on the actions that will move us closer to our goals. When we know what we want to achieve, we can prioritize our tasks and make decisions that align with our long-term vision.

2. **Motivation:** Having a clear sense of our desired destiny serves as a powerful source of motivation. It gives us something to strive for, inspiring us to push through challenges and setbacks on our journey. When we can visualize our ultimate goal, we are more likely to stay committed and persevere in the face of obstacles.

3. **Alignment with Values:** Clarity of our desired destiny allows us to align our goals with our core values and beliefs. When our actions are in harmony with our values, we experience a deeper sense of fulfillment and authenticity in our lives. This alignment also helps us make decisions that are in line with our true selves.

4. **Effective Planning:** Knowing our desired destiny enables us to create a roadmap for achieving our goals. With a clear destination in mind, we can set specific, measurable objectives and develop actionable plans to reach them. This strategic approach increases our chances of success and minimizes wasted time and resources.

5. **Sense of Purpose:** Clarity of our desired destiny gives our lives a sense of purpose and meaning. When we have a clear vision for our future, every step we take feels purposeful and intentional. This sense of purpose provides us with a sense of direction and fulfillment, enriching our overall quality of life.

6. **Resilience:** Knowing our desired destiny makes us more resilient in the face of adversity. When we encounter challenges or setbacks, our clear vision of the future helps us maintain perspective and stay focused on our long-term goals. This resilience allows us to bounce back from setbacks and continue moving forward with determination.

Having clarity of our desired destiny is essential for achieving success, fulfillment, and personal growth. It provides us with focus, motivation, and direction, allowing us to align our actions with our values and make meaningful progress towards our goals. By defining our desired destiny, we can create a roadmap for success and live with purpose and intentionality.

As an advocate for hands-on learning and experiential teaching methods, I wholeheartedly suggest engaging in any of the following three activities to help define your North Star and clarify your goals:

1. **Vision Board Creation:** A vision board is a powerful visualization tool that allows you to visually represent your aspirations and goals. To create a vision board, gather magazines, images, quotes, and other materials that resonate with your dreams and aspirations.
Then, arrange these elements on a board or poster, creating a collage that reflects your desired future. By immersing yourself in this creative process, you'll gain clarity on your goals and manifest your aspirations into reality.
2. **Affirmation Writing:** Affirmations are positive statements that affirm your desired outcomes and beliefs. Take some time to reflect on your goals and

aspirations, then write out affirmations that align with these objectives. For example, if your goal is to advance in your career, you might write affirmations such as "I am confident in my abilities and deserving of success," or "I attract opportunities for growth and advancement." By regularly reciting these affirmations, you'll reinforce positive beliefs and align your thoughts and actions with your desired outcomes.

3. **Mind Mapping:** Mind mapping is a creative technique for visualizing connections between ideas and concepts. Start by writing your main goal or aspiration in the center of a blank page. Then, branch out from this central point, adding related ideas, subgoals, and action steps in a hierarchical structure. Use lines, colors, and images to connect and organize your thoughts. Mind mapping allows you to explore different aspects of your goal and identify potential paths to achieving it.

By engaging in these activities, you'll gain clarity and focus on your North Star, enabling you to take meaningful steps towards realizing your dreams. Remember, the journey towards your goals is as important as the destination, and these activities will help you stay motivated and inspired along the way.

But wait, what occurs when inspiration evades us? When self-doubt creeps in, and the nagging voice questions our abilities and the feasibility of our goals? In such moments of uncertainty, it's essential to acknowledge the validity of these feelings while also recognizing that they do not define our trajectory. Instead, we can turn to activities that nurture our happiness and well-being, restoring our sense of balance and **reigniting our inner spark.**

CHAPTER 1: DARE TO DREAM

What can I do to reignite my inner spark? Here are some examples of simple activities that you may want to consider; but ultimately, it is your choice.

Consider the simple yet profound act of **baking**—a therapeutic endeavor that engages our senses, stimulates creativity, and fosters a sense of accomplishment. The rhythmic kneading of dough, the aroma of freshly baked goods wafting through the air—these sensory experiences can serve as a welcome respite from the noise of self-doubt, grounding us in the present moment and reigniting our passion for life.

Alternatively, **dancing** offers a liberating outlet for self-expression, allowing us to release pent-up emotions and embrace the joy of movement. Whether dancing alone in the privacy of our home or joining a group class, the act of dancing can uplift our spirits, boost our confidence, and remind us of the sheer exhilaration of being alive.

Meditation provides another invaluable tool for navigating moments of uncertainty and self-doubt. By quieting the mind and turning inward, we can cultivate a sense of inner peace and clarity, gaining perspective on our challenges and accessing our innate reservoir of strength and resilience.

For those who seek solace in nature, a leisurely **bike ride** offers an opportunity to connect with the outdoors, soak in the beauty of the natural world, and experience a profound sense of freedom and serenity. The rhythmic motion of pedaling, the gentle breeze against our skin—it's a reminder of life's inherent beauty and the limitless possibilities that lie ahead.

Of course, indulging in a **hot tub bath** provides a luxurious escape from the stresses of daily life, enveloping us in warmth and relaxation. As we soak away our worries, we create space for introspection and self-care, rejuvenating both body and soul.

Even seemingly mundane tasks like **cleaning or folding**

laundry can offer moments of solace and satisfaction. Engaging in these activities mindfully, we find a sense of order and accomplishment in the completion of small tasks—a reminder that progress, however incremental, is still progress.

Ultimately, the key lies in honoring our emotions, embracing self-compassion, and finding solace in activities that bring us joy and fulfillment. In doing so, we cultivate resilience, nurture our well-being, and reclaim our sense of purpose and inspiration.

As we approach the culmination of this chapter towards realizing our dreams, it's crucial to fortify our aspirations with a deep understanding of our strengths and the essence of our true selves. This final step entails peeling back the layers to reveal our authentic identities—the qualities, talents, and characteristics that make us uniquely special.

Identifying our strengths is similar to uncovering hidden treasures within ourselves. These are the innate abilities and talents that empower us to navigate life's challenges and seize opportunities with confidence and purpose. Whether it's our creativity, resilience, empathy, or problem-solving skills, acknowledging and leveraging our strengths provides a solid foundation upon which to build our dreams.

Moreover, unmasking our true selves involves embracing the full spectrum of our identities and experiences. It's about honoring our quirks, passions, and values without reservation or apology. What sets us apart from others is not our conformity to societal norms but rather our authenticity—the unfiltered expression of our true essence.

In this process of self-discovery, we may uncover aspects of ourselves that have long remained dormant or unrecognized. Perhaps it's a hidden talent for storytelling, a passion for social justice, or a talent for bringing people together. By shining a light on these unique attributes, we not only gain a deeper understanding of ourselves but also unlock the door to boundless possibilities and potential. **What are the qualities that you are known for?**

    Furthermore, recognizing our uniqueness fosters a sense of self-worth and empowerment. When we embrace our individuality, we liberate ourselves from the constraints of comparison and self-doubt, allowing our light to shine brightly in the world. After all, it is our authenticity that enables us to forge meaningful connections, make a lasting impact, and fulfill our highest potential.

    Reinforcing our dreams with a deep appreciation of our strengths and true selves is the final step towards actualizing our aspirations. By embracing our unique qualities and staying true to ourselves, we not only set ourselves up for success but also pave the way for a life filled with purpose, fulfillment, and authenticity.

Chapter 2
MAKE A PLAN

Charting Your Course: Crafting a Strategic Plan for Dream Achievement

In Chapter 1, I mentioned the importance of having a North Star to guide us in the direction of our dreams. In this chapter we will dive into the benefit of having a comprehensive plan to navigate life's endeavors successfully. Reflecting on my journey, one of my earliest aspirations was to shatter the generational cycle within my family by obtaining a college degree. However, this was just the tip of the iceberg. As I ventured into my thirties, three significant dreams converged: homeownership, motherhood, and professional advancement. Each dream necessitated its own unique roadmap, yet they were all intricately intertwined, influencing one another's trajectory.

Let's revisit the previous chapter where I shared my fervent desire to attain a college education. This journey spanned six years, fraught with challenges and valuable lessons. It's imperative to underscore the significance of clarity, understanding one's passions, and leveraging strengths. Without these guiding principles, one risks veering off-course, as I did, losing precious time. Nevertheless, I am here to share my experiences, helping to clarify the path to success.

Embarking on community college, I lacked role models or familial guidance. Thankfully, my mother's intern, offered assistance with course selection and enrollment. Despite his best intentions, his advice steered me towards a track in Business Administration. While initially this aligned with my aspirations of corporate employment, I soon discovered a profound conflict with the coursework and a dislike of courses like Business Law, Accounting, Computer Science, and others. Balancing full-time employment to help my mom pay for her home and school enrollment in the United States while crossing the border daily from Mexico proved daunting; after three arduous years, progress remained intangible.

Complicating matters, my decision to marry Paco and

move south of Mexico led me to put my education on hold temporarily. Upon relocating to Mexico City and later the United States, I faced a lack of direction, allowing circumstances to dictate my trajectory. It wasn't until I reached a critical juncture at twenty-six, where the latent desires of motherhood and homeownership began to surface, that I realized the need for proactive planning.

Fueled by this epiphany, I meticulously crafted a **personal timeline,** delineating the requisite steps for academic advancement. However, it was a serendipitous comment from my husband that catalyzed a pivotal shift in my academic pursuits. Challenging my preconceived notions, he suggested a major change to Psychology, recognizing my affinity for interpersonal dynamics. Skeptical yet intrigued, I enrolled in Psychology 101 and discovered my true passion, prompting a swift transition in majors.

With newfound clarity, I embraced the Specific, Measurable, Achievable, Relevant, and Time-Bound (SMART) method of goal-setting methodology, prioritizing flexibility and financial stability. Upon recognizing the urgency to steer my life towards a more fulfilling trajectory, I wasted no time in embarking on a job search. Remarkably, I stumbled upon a position that would serve as the cornerstone of my corporate career journey. I secured employment as a disability claim specialist, a role that entrusted me with the pivotal responsibility of managing a caseload of disability claims and overseeing the claims process.

What made this opportunity truly transformative was its alignment with my overarching goals. Notably, the job boasted a flexible schedule, enabling me to pursue my educational aspirations concurrently. I would commence my workday as early as 7 a.m., concluding by 3:30 p.m., thereby affording me the precious window from 5 p.m. to 9 p.m. to attend classes at a local university.

In my quest to understand the educational landscape and identify an institution that complimented my learning style, I conducted thorough research on local public universities. Coincidentally, I discovered that California State University Los Angeles offered a trimester approach, which resonated profoundly with my preferences. The condensed yet intensive class structure spanned ten-week periods, a stark contrast to the conventional eighteen-week semester model. This format suited my learning style admirably, facilitating a more focused and efficient academic experience.

Moreover, the stars seemed to align as my new job presented an invaluable perk: tuition reimbursement. This unforeseen blessing not only alleviated the financial strain of pursuing higher education but also underscored the employer's commitment to employee development. With this support in hand, I embarked on my educational journey with renewed vigor, and excited about the prospect of professional growth and personal fulfillment.

Furthermore, the financial aspect of my employment situation underwent a positive transformation. Not only did my new role offer the flexibility I craved and facilitate my academic pursuits, but it also provided a slightly higher income compared to my previous position at an insurance agency. This uptick in earnings, coupled with the financial aid of tuition reimbursement, laid the groundwork for our long-awaited dream of homeownership, signaling a significant step towards financial stability and independence.

In essence, the combination of a flexible work schedule, tailored educational opportunities, tuition reimbursement, and improved financial prospects positioned me on a trajectory of unprecedented growth and advancement. This pivotal juncture marked the commencement of a transformative chapter in my life, characterized by relentless pursuit of personal and professional excellence, and the realization of long-held aspirations.

CHAPTER 2: MAKE A PLAN

Armed with these resources, I charted a course towards academic achievement and financial independence.

Simultaneously, the dream of homeownership began to materialize. Despite humble beginnings in a converted garage, we diligently saved and our strategic planning culminated in the purchase of our first home, a testament to resilience and determination.

As I approached the culmination of my academic journey, I found myself embarking on a transformative phase in my professional life. Recognizing the need to stretch beyond my comfort zone, I delved into understanding the intricate landscape of career opportunities available to me. Having recently achieved a significant milestone—a promotion from Disability Benefit Specialist (DBS) to Senior DBS—I thirsted for further growth and advancement.

The next logical step in my career progression beckoned—to transition into a consultant role. However, I understood that this endeavor required more than just aspiration; it demanded a distinct differentiation from my peers. To excel in this capacity, I needed to demonstrate expertise across multiple domains, while adeptly navigating job aids and standard operating procedures. This realization underscored the importance of clarity regarding my desired destination and the strategic leveraging of my strengths.

Amidst the cubicle office environment, an outstanding observation emerged. My English-speaking colleagues often coped with frustration when compelled to enlist Spanish translators during their interactions with claimants. Particularly during intricate initial interviews requiring detailed information such as upcoming doctor appointments, medication regimens, and therapy sessions, the reliance on translation services became apparent. It was here that I experienced a revelation—a profound "aha" moment.

Recognizing my proficiency in Spanish, I proposed a solution to my manager. By assuming responsibility for all Spanish-speaking calls and managing claims in Spanish, I not only enhanced the quality of service but also eliminated the need for external translation services, thereby yielding cost savings for the organization. Thus, I forged a new role for myself—that of a bilingual Senior DBS. In this capacity, I not only added value to claim management but also showcased my ability to innovate and contribute tangibly to organizational efficiency.

Yet, amidst these milestones, the desire for motherhood was starting to occupy my mind and my heart, and as I got closer to the finish line of obtaining a bachelor's degree, I knew deep inside this was now the right time. Leveraging the **backward design,** I meticulously orchestrated the timing to coincide with my imminent graduation. Blessed with a seamless pregnancy, I welcomed motherhood with open arms, completing the trifecta of achievement at the age of thirty.

Lifted by this success, I set my sights on the next milestone: I was notified that upon my return from maternity leave, I was to assume the role of mentor to incoming trainees. This decision not only aligned with my passion for teaching but also synergized seamlessly with my newfound expertise in disability claims management. By embracing challenges, leveraging my strengths, and fostering innovation, I navigated the landscape of career progression with determination and purpose, setting the stage for continued success and fulfillment in the years to come.

But our lives are not just about school and work. My husband and I shared a dream: we wanted to create lasting memories by exploring the world. We dreamed of visiting places we had only seen in books, magazines, travel brochures, or TV documentaries. So, since we got married, we made travel a priority. Every year, we aim to visit a new city, country, or place, and sometimes we manage to go to more than one destination in a year. As a result, we dedicate time in November and December of every year to begin the planning of the following year's vacations during spring break and summer.

To make this happen, we had to plan carefully. We used the **understanding of the landscape approach.** We needed to save money, check school vacation dates, request time off from work, arrange transportation to the airport, and always hunt for the best deals. With this dedication, over our thirty years of marriage, we have traveled to over twenty countries, including Iceland, Italy, Spain, Argentina, Brazil, and many more. We also have taken local trips to national parks, amusement parks, and beautiful beaches.

This approach to achieving our travel dreams can be applied to anything you want to accomplish. Whether your goal is big or small, it requires effort and planning. Your heart and mind guide you to what you want to achieve, so don't be afraid to pursue your desires with the same dedication.

In the subsequent chapter, I will delve into the intricacies of home selection and the journey towards home ownership, underscoring the resilience and fortitude that propelled me forward. Below, I present a comprehensive breakdown of the five methods I employed to successfully achieve my primary goals during my thirties: completing my college education, purchasing a home, starting a family, traveling, and securing a promotion. It is my sincere hope that you find these strategies enlightening and practical, empowering you to pursue your own aspirations with confidence and determination:

A) **Understanding the landscape** or conducting research is a crucial step in any endeavor, whether it's pursuing education, career advancement, or personal goals like traveling. Here's an explanation of what it entails along with some details on how to execute it effectively:

1. **Define Your Objective:** Before delving into research, clearly define your objective. Whether it's choosing a college major, finding a job, or planning a business venture, knowing what you aim to achieve will guide your research efforts.
2. **Gather Information:** Start by gathering relevant information from various sources. These could include:
    - **Online Resources:** Utilize search engines, educational websites, and professional networks to gather information related to your objective.
    - **Books and Publications:** Look for books, academic journals, magazines, and industry publications that offer insights into your area of interest.
    - **Expert Advice:** Seek guidance from professionals, mentors, or individuals with experience in your field. Their insights can be invaluable in shaping your understanding.
    - **Surveys and Interviews:** Conduct surveys or interviews with experts or individuals who have pursued similar paths to gain firsthand insights and advice.
3. **Analyze and Synthesize:** Once you have gathered information, analyze and synthesize it to draw meaningful conclusions. Look for patterns, trends, and key insights that can inform your decision-making process.
4. **Consider Various Perspectives**: It's essential to consider multiple perspectives and viewpoints during your research. This ensures a well-rounded understanding of the landscape and helps you anticipate potential challenges or opportunities.

5. **Evaluate Resources and Constraints:** Assess the resources available to you, including time, finances, and support networks. Consider any constraints or limitations that may impact your ability to pursue your objectives.

6. **Stay Updated:** Keep abreast of current developments, trends, and changes in your field of interest. Continuous learning and staying updated will ensure that your understanding of the landscape remains relevant and informed.

7. **Seek Feedback:** Finally, seek feedback on your research findings and conclusions. Share your insights with trusted advisors, mentors, or peers to gain additional perspectives and refine your understanding further.

By following these steps and approaching research with diligence and curiosity, you can gain a comprehensive understanding of the landscape surrounding your objectives, enabling you to make informed decisions and navigate your path effectively.

B) **A personal timeline** is a strategic tool used to plan and organize individual goals, milestones, and tasks within a specific timeframe. It serves as a roadmap for personal and professional development, helping individuals stay focused, motivated, and accountable. Here's an explanation along with some details on how to create and utilize a personal timeline effectively:

1. **Identify Goals and Objectives:** Begin by identifying your overarching goals and objectives. These could be related to education, career, relationships, health, or any other aspect of your life that you want to focus on.

2. **Break Down Goals into Milestones**: Once you've identified your goals, break them down into smaller, achievable milestones. These milestones serve as checkpoints along your journey, helping you track progress and stay motivated.

3. **Set Timeframes:** Assign realistic timeframes to each milestone based on your priorities, resources, and constraints. Be specific about when you aim to achieve each milestone, whether it's weeks, months, or years into the future.

4. **Prioritize Tasks:** Within each milestone, identify the specific tasks or actions required to achieve it. Prioritize these tasks based on their importance and urgency, focusing on high-impact activities that contribute directly to your goals.

5. **Allocate Resources:** Assess the resources needed to accomplish each task, including time, money, skills, and support. Allocate resources accordingly, making adjustments as needed to ensure feasibility and success.

6. **Create a Visual Timeline:** Organize your milestones and tasks into a visual timeline, such as a calendar, Gantt chart, or project management software. This allows you to see your progress at a glance and stay on track with deadlines.

7. **Review and Adjust Regularly:** Regularly review your personal timeline to track progress, identify obstacles, and make adjustments as needed. Be flexible and responsive to changes in circumstances, priorities, or goals.

8. **Stay Accountable:** Hold yourself accountable for sticking to your timeline and completing tasks on schedule. Consider sharing your timeline with a mentor, coach, or accountability partner who can provide support and encouragement along the way.

9. **Celebrate Achievements:** Celebrate your successes and milestones along the journey. Acknowledge your progress and use it as motivation to continue moving forward towards your goals.
10. **Reflect and Iterate:** Periodically reflect on your experiences, lessons learned, and areas for improvement. Use this feedback to iterate and refine your personal timeline, ensuring that it remains relevant and effective in guiding your journey.

By creating a personal timeline and following these steps, you can effectively plan, prioritize, and achieve your goals, fostering personal growth and fulfillment along the way.

C) SMART goal setting is a methodology created by George T. Doran, Arthur Miller, and James Cunningham in the 1980s, but that continues to be extremely relevant. Here's an explanation of each component along with some details on how to apply SMART goal setting effectively:

1. **Specific:** Goals should be clear, specific, and well-defined. They answer the questions: What do you want to accomplish? Why is it important? Who is involved? Where will it take place? By defining goals with precision, you eliminate ambiguity and increase clarity, making it easier to focus and take action.

Example: Instead of setting a vague goal like "Improve my fitness," a specific goal would be "Run a 5k race in under 30 minutes by the end of the year."

2. **Measurable:** Goals should include criteria for measuring progress and success. They answer the question: How will you know when you've achieved your goal? By establishing measurable criteria, you can track your progress, stay motivated, and make informed decisions about your actions.

Example: Using the previous goal of running a 5k race, measurable criteria could include tracking weekly running mileage, monitoring pace improvements, or recording race times in training runs.

3. **Achievable**: Goals should be realistic and attainable given your resources, capabilities, and constraints. They answer the question: Is the goal within reach, given current circumstances? Setting achievable goals helps prevent frustration and discouragement, while still challenging you to stretch beyond your comfort zone.

Example: If you're currently running a 5k in 40 minutes, setting a goal to run a 5k in under 20 minutes within a month may not be achievable. However, setting a goal to gradually improve your race time by 1-2 minutes each month could be more realistic.

4. **Relevant:** Goals should be relevant and aligned with your values, priorities, and long-term objectives. They answer the question: Does the goal matter to you and contribute to your overall objectives? By ensuring relevance, you maintain focus and motivation, maximizing your chances of success.

Example: If your long-term objective is to improve overall health and well-being, a relevant goal could be to incorporate strength training into your fitness routine to prevent injury and improve performance in running.

5. **Time-bound:** Goals should have a defined timeline or deadline for completion. They answer the question: When will you achieve the goal? Setting time-bound goals creates a sense of urgency, provides a framework for planning, and helps prevent procrastination.

Example: Adding a deadline to the previous goal, you could specify: "Run a 5k race in under 30 minutes by December 31 of this year."

By applying the SMART criteria to goal setting, you can create goals that are specific, measurable, achievable, relevant, and time-bound, increasing your likelihood of success and empowering you to make meaningful progress towards your aspirations.

D) **Backward Design was introduced in 1949 by Ralph W. Tyler, an American educator, when discussing statements of objectives. However, educators and authors Grant Wiggins and Jay McTighe popularized the concept in their 1998 book** *Understanding by Design.* **Backward design, also known as backward planning or backward mapping,** is a strategic approach used to envision and plan for future outcomes by projecting oneself ahead in time and working backward to identify the steps needed to achieve a desired goal or outcome. Here's an explanation of the methodology along with some details on how to apply it effectively:

1. **Envision the Future:** Begin by visualizing the desired future outcome or goal you want to achieve. This could be anything from completing a project, reaching a milestone, or realizing a long-term aspiration.

2. **Set a Future Date:** Determine a specific date or timeframe by which you aim to achieve the desired outcome. This serves as the endpoint or target for your planning process.

3. **Work Backward:** Once you have established the future date, mentally "leap forward" to that point in time and imagine that the goal has been successfully achieved. Then, work backward from that future point to identify the steps and milestones necessary to reach that outcome.

4. **Identify Milestones and Tasks:** Break down the journey from the future date to the present into smaller, manageable milestones and tasks. These could include deadlines, checkpoints, actions, or achievements that need to be accomplished along the way.

5. **Sequence the Steps:** Arrange the milestones and tasks in chronological order, ensuring that each step logically leads to the next and contributes to the overall progression toward the desired outcome.

6. **Allocate Resources and Time:** Assess the resources, skills, and time required to accomplish each milestone and task. Allocate resources effectively, considering constraints such as budget, availability, and capacity.

7. **Create a Plan:** Develop a detailed plan or timeline that outlines the sequence of activities, deadlines, responsibilities, and dependencies. This plan serves as a roadmap for executing the steps needed to achieve the desired outcome.

8. **Monitor Progress:** Regularly monitor and track progress toward the goal, adjusting the plan as necessary based on changes in circumstances, priorities, or constraints. Celebrate achievements and milestones along the way to maintain motivation and momentum.

9. **Stay Flexible:** Remain flexible and adaptable throughout the planning and implementation process. Unexpected challenges or opportunities may arise, requiring adjustments to the plan to ensure continued progress toward the desired outcome.

10. **Take Action:** Finally, take action and begin executing the plan, starting with the first milestone or task. Stay committed, focused, and disciplined as you work through the steps toward achieving the envisioned future outcome.

By employing the backward goal setting, individuals can effectively plan for future outcomes by envisioning success, working backward to identify the necessary steps, and taking action to bring their goals to fruition. This strategic approach helps to clarify objectives, prioritize activities, and maintain momentum toward achieving desired outcomes.

E) **Tuition reimbursement** is often considered a lifeline for employees seeking to further their education while maintaining employment. This benefit, offered by many companies, provides financial assistance to employees pursuing educational courses or degrees relevant to their job or career advancement. Here are some fictitious scenarios and people that help illustrate why tuition reimbursement is seen as a lifeline:

1. **Financial Support:** One of the most significant benefits of tuition reimbursement is the financial assistance it provides. Pursuing higher education can be expensive, with tuition fees, textbooks, and other expenses adding up quickly. Tuition reimbursement helps alleviate the financial burden by covering some or all of these costs, making education more accessible and affordable for employees.

Example: Sarah, a customer service representative, wants to advance her career by obtaining a degree in business administration. However, she is hesitant to enroll in college due to the high tuition fees. Fortunately, her employer offers tuition reimbursement, allowing her to pursue her degree without worrying about the financial implications.

2. **Professional Development:** Tuition reimbursement encourages employees to invest in their professional development and acquire new skills or qualifications that are relevant to their job or industry. By supporting ongoing education, employers can cultivate a skilled and knowledgeable workforce, ultimately benefiting the company's performance and competitiveness.

Example: John works in the information technology (IT) department of a software company. His employer offers tuition reimbursement for courses related to technology and programming. John decides to enroll in a coding bootcamp to enhance his skills in web development, knowing that it will benefit both his career and the company.

3. **Retention and Loyalty:** Providing tuition reimbursement can enhance employee satisfaction and loyalty by demonstrating that the company values its employees'

personal and professional growth. Employees are more likely to stay with an employer that invests in their development, reducing turnover and retention costs for the company.

Example: Emily has been working for a marketing agency for several years. She considers leaving the company to pursue a higher-paying job elsewhere. However, she decides to stay after learning about the company's tuition reimbursement program, which will help her pursue a master's degree in marketing while continuing to work.

4. **Skill Acquisition and Talent Development:** Tuition reimbursement programs enable employees to acquire new skills or qualifications that are in demand in the job market. By investing in employee training and development, employers can attract top talent and foster a culture of continuous learning and innovation.

Example: James, an entry-level engineer, wants to specialize in renewable energy technologies. His employer offers tuition reimbursement for courses related to sustainable engineering. James takes advantage of this opportunity to enroll in a certificate program on solar energy systems, enhancing his expertise in this emerging field.

Overall, tuition reimbursement serves as a lifeline for employees seeking to advance their careers through education, providing financial support, fostering professional development, enhancing retention and loyalty, and promoting skill acquisition and talent development. By investing in their employees' education, employers can create a win-win situation that benefits both the individual and the organization.

Achieving my primary goals during my thirties required a combination of strategic planning, continuous learning, financial management, adaptability, and seeking support from my network. By embracing these methods and applying them diligently, I was able to realize my aspirations and create a fulfilling life for myself and my family. I encourage you to embrace these strategies and embark on your own journey towards achieving your dreams with confidence and determination.

What is the short answer to all of the above or how would I summarize this chapter in TWO words? **TAKE ACTION!**

1. **Overcoming Inertia:** Often, the biggest obstacle to achieving our goals is simply getting started. Taking action breaks the inertia and initiates momentum towards progress. Without that initial step, we risk stagnation and complacency, hindering our growth and development.
2. **Building Confidence:** By taking action, we demonstrate our commitment and belief in our ability to succeed. Each small step forward builds confidence and reinforces our belief that we are capable of achieving our goals. This confidence propels us to take further action and tackle more significant challenges.
3. **Gaining Clarity:** Taking action allows us to gain valuable insights and feedback that we wouldn't otherwise have. It provides clarity on what works and what doesn't, enabling us to adjust our approach and refine our strategies as needed. Through action, we learn and adapt, moving closer to our objectives with each iteration.
4. **Creating Momentum:** Action begets action. Once we take that initial step, it becomes easier to continue moving forward. Momentum builds as we gain traction

and make progress towards our goals. Even small actions can snowball into significant achievements over time, fueling our motivation and drive.

5. **Seizing Opportunities:** Opportunities rarely come to those who wait; they must be actively pursued. By taking action, we position ourselves to capitalize on opportunities as they arise. Whether it's seizing a chance to learn a new skill, explore a new opportunity, or overcome a challenge, proactive action opens doors to new possibilities and experiences.

6. **Avoiding Regret:** Taking action prevents us from looking back with regret and wondering "What if?" Regret often stems from missed opportunities and unfulfilled potential. By taking action and pursuing our goals wholeheartedly, we minimize the likelihood of regret and instead create a life filled with purpose, fulfillment, and satisfaction.

Chapter 3
STICK TO THE PLAN

Navigating Challenges with Determination

Throughout my life, I have found that the most impactful outcomes have always been a part of a well-thought-out plan. This principle has held true from my academic pursuits, to significant financial milestones, experiencing the joy of becoming a parent three times, and navigating through a career that demanded relocating across various countries and states. These achievements didn't happen by chance; they were the fruits of meticulous planning and unwavering dedication.

As I have mentioned in earlier chapters, achieving success and reaching our desired goals necessitates dreaming big. It requires us to craft a clear vision of our future, one that is not only envisioned but also articulated in writing. This vision must be meticulously broken down into manageable steps and specific, actionable items that lead to defined outcomes.

However, life is inherently unpredictable—filled with its highs and lows, triumphs and setbacks. On this journey, one might wonder how to stay committed to their dreams amidst the complexities of daily life. This is where our character truly shines—through self-discipline and faith, traits that empower us to advance, albeit gradually, moving the needle forward one step at a time, one day at a time.

The extraordinary stories of individuals who have achieved remarkable success underscore this point. Take Arnold Schwarzenegger, for instance, whose dreams didn't just stop at becoming the world's best bodybuilder with multiple Mr. Universe and Mr. Olympia titles to his name. He pivoted from sports to a successful career in politics, serving two terms as the governor of California. Then there's Madam C.J. Walker, America's first self-made female millionaire, who revolutionized the beauty industry for African American women with her innovative direct sales model that also focused on empowering and educating women. Or consider José Hernández, a Mexican American engineer and former NASA astronaut, who transitioned from working in California's agricultural fields to traveling in space, inspired by the moon landing he watched as a child. These stories, each unique and inspiring, have shown me the power of perseverance and vision.

While I may not have reached such towering levels of impact yet, I draw immense inspiration from these narratives. They remind me—and hopefully will remind you—of the importance of sticking to a strategic plan, even when faced with adversity. In sharing my personal experiences, I aim to connect these broader concepts with real-life applications, offering practical strategies that you can adapt and employ in your own journey. Think of these strategies as a menu of options, each tailored to help keep you motivated and on track toward achieving your dreams. Whether it's setting incremental goals, maintaining a positive mindset, or leveraging your support network, the key is to find what works best for you and to persist with confidence and determination. By embracing these principles and methods, we not only navigate the complexities of life but also shape our destinies, one deliberate step at a time.

Story No. 1: Our First Home and the Power of Vision and Faith

In the previous chapters, I've shared glimpses of our humble beginnings when my husband and I arrived in the United States with less than a thousand dollars and dreams packed into two suitcases. During our first five years, we resided in a converted car garage—a modest, makeshift home that fueled my longing for something as simple, yet significant, as a one-bedroom apartment. However, my husband had grander visions that extended far beyond my immediate desires.

One evening, as we were returning from work, my husband pointed out a complex of newly constructed townhomes in

Pasadena, California, our city of residence at the time. He casually mentioned the possibility of us owning a property there, planting the early seeds of a dream I thought far beyond our reach. At that time, the idea of purchasing a home seemed as complex and foreign as the new country we were trying to navigate. Between my full-time job and school commitments, the prospect felt distant, yet we agreed to continue saving for a down payment, despite not knowing the exact requirements or the additional costs involved.

Over the years, as we pursued our American dream, we found ourselves working relentlessly—my husband often clocking in 72-hour weeks across two jobs, while I balanced full-time employment with my studies. Despite our hectic schedules, we managed to indulge in modest travels, from San Francisco and Hawaii to international destinations like Jamaica, Brazil, and Canada, which enriched our lives and expanded our horizons.

On New Year's Day 2000, a visit to the Rosewalk townhome community unexpectedly deepened our aspirations. The sight of the gated enclave, with its lush landscapes and communal amenities, like a swimming pool, seemed out of reach. Standing outside, I battled my doubts, questioning the feasibility of such a dream. Yet, inspired by my husband's unwavering determination, I began to entertain the possibility: Why couldn't we, hardworking and goal-oriented, live here?

Our previous aspirations had led us to invest in vehicles—a new Volkswagen Beetle, a luxurious Land Rover, and a previously owned Alfa Romeo, reflecting our progress and growing financial stability. It was early 2001 when my husband spotted a for-sale sign at Rosewalk. Seizing the moment, we contacted the listed agent late at night and set an appointment that would set us on an unforeseen path.

Visiting the property, we learned on the spot about

the necessity of having our own real estate agent. Quickly, we found one, inexperienced yet eager, which turned to our advantage amidst a competitive market. We faced a significant hurdle when we realized we were short $5,000 to cover all down payments and closing costs—a sum that would deplete our savings entirely.

In a twist of fate, a car accident involving the Alfa Romeo, which initially seemed like a setback, transformed into an unexpected financial godsend. The car was totaled, but the insurance valuation and subsequent purchase of the damaged vehicle to then resell it not only covered the shortfall but also provided the exact amount needed to finalize our home purchase. And we still had two other vehicles, so no extra expense was incurred!

The final piece fell into place when the seller proposed a unique arrangement: she would pay us the equivalent of a month's mortgage payment as rent to remain in the home while transitioning to her new residence. This offer alleviated our immediate financial burden, allowing us to make our first mortgage payment.

In June 2001, we moved into our new home in Rosewalk, a tangible manifestation of our dreams and proof of our perseverance. This journey taught us the invaluable lesson that with a clear vision, unwavering faith, and resolute **determination,** even seemingly insurmountable obstacles can be overcome. This experience wasn't just about acquiring property—it was about learning to navigate the complexities of life with optimism and resilience, guided by a belief in a higher power and the abundance it brings. Through this, we learned that life's challenges are merely stepping stones to achieving greater heights.

Story No. 2: Becoming the Head of the Department

I still vividly remember my entry into corporate America at the age of 28. Fresh from transitioning to a full-time student role at a local university, I began my corporate journey as a disability benefit specialist, the most foundational position within my organization. It was here that I first encountered one of the most influential tools in my early professional career—a detailed "Career Path" guide. This guide meticulously outlined the necessary skills, metrics, and behaviors required to advance to higher roles within the department, culminating at the Consultant level, which was characterized by its technical demands. In addition, I had a wonderful manager who not only led by example but also expected the highest levels of excellence and under her leadership, I have experienced the most challenging yet rewarding opportunities. It takes one person to believe in us for us to turn into fearless motivated dreamers. I will always be in debt to her for positioning me into the right roles.

Eager to progress, I kept a copy of the career path in my cubicle and diligently crafted a plan to meet each criterion for advancement. By the time I had ascended to the role of Senior Disability Specialist, I was already strategizing my next move toward becoming a Consultant. I used the time in my one-to-one meetings to discuss my plans with my manager and to ensure I was asking for timely feedback. I recall sharing with my colleagues my ambition to become the Head of the Department by the age of forty. While some were skeptical, I remained undeterred, often envisioning myself in the corner office that I would one day occupy.

During this time of professional growth, my personal life also was flourishing. In 2001, my husband and I bought our first house. I graduated with a bachelor's in Psychology from

CHAPTER 3: STICK TO THE PLAN

California State University, Los Angeles, in 2002, the same year we welcomed our first son. By 2003, with my career trajectory firmly in mind, I set a new educational goal—to pursue a master's degree through an accelerated program tailored for working professionals. This program needed to be local, not require the Graduate Record Examinations (GRE), and focus on business without the heavy financial coursework typical of an MBA.

I discovered the perfect program at a nearby private university. However, knowing myself well enough to recognize my need for a support system, and an **"accountability buddy,"** I recruited my mentor, a bright and dedicated colleague whose alma mater was my chosen university. She had previously expressed interest in pursuing a master's, and after some persuasion, agreed to join me. We would carpool from my house, making the most of the carpool lanes during California's peak traffic hours, and for the twenty months that followed, we only missed one session due to unforeseen circumstances.

Balancing this rigorous academic schedule with work and family life was no small feat. My typical week was a carefully orchestrated routine:

- **Monday:** A full day of work followed by classes from 6 p.m. to 10 p.m.
- **Tuesday:** Work all day, then home to manage household chores.
- **Wednesday:** After work, I would start reading the required chapters for the week.
- **Thursday:** Another full day of work, then beginning outlines for next Monday's essay.
- **Friday:** Work until the afternoon, then time off to unwind with friends and family.

- **Saturday:** My marathon study day, starting at 5 a.m. and breaking intermittently to care for my son, resuming when my husband returned from work.
- **Sunday:** Grocery shopping and meal prep for the week, along with finalizing any academic assignments.

This disciplined schedule enabled me to graduate with a Master's in Organizational Management in May 2005. I continued to excel at work, focusing on leadership development, internal branding, and continuously stepping out of my comfort zone—all with the ultimate goal of becoming the head of the department.

My journey was punctuated by personal challenges, including a life-threatening complication during my second son's birth in late 2006, which resulted in post-partum eclampsia. Despite these hurdles, **I persevered** both personally and professionally.

Upon learning of an opening for the head of the department during my second maternity leave, I did not hesitate to express my interest, even though I knew it was two levels higher than the manager role that I had at that point. The role initially went on hold due to restructuring at the executive level, but this delay serendipitously aligned with my return from leave. When the role was reopened, now listed at an assistant vice president (AVP) level, I faced stiff competition from colleagues at the director level. Despite their doubts and my own fears, I applied, backed by a comprehensive portfolio and a clear demonstration of my growth and capabilities.

After an intense series of interviews and a suspenseful wait, I was chosen for the role, albeit with an adjustment to director II to accommodate HR guidelines. At 36, I achieved my goal, marking a significant milestone in a journey that began at the entry-level. This success was not just a testament to my **determination and self-discipline** but also to the power of having a supportive network of mentors and managers, a theme I will explore further in Chapter 7.

As a final thought for this chapter, and as I have shared in all my HISPA school presentations, "When in fear, grab the bull by the horns." It is inevitable to feel fear at any given point during our pursuit, and we must learn to manage it. When faced with fear, the best approach is to grab the bull by the horns and move forward with determination. Fear can be paralyzing, creating a mental barrier that prevents progress and stifles potential. By confronting fear head-on, we take control of the situation, transforming anxiety into action and uncertainty into opportunity. This courageous stance not only diminishes the power of fear but also builds resilience and confidence, proving to ourselves that we are capable of overcoming challenges. Embracing fear in this way allows us to grow, learn, and ultimately achieve our goals with a sense of accomplishment and empowerment.

Now, as promised for every chapter, three practical methodologies to help you **stick to the plan.**

ACCOUNTABILITY BUDDY

An accountability buddy is a powerful tool for achieving personal and professional goals. This relationship is built on mutual support, encouragement, and commitment to holding each other accountable for specific objectives. Whether the goals are related to fitness, education, career advancement, or personal growth, an accountability buddy can significantly enhance your motivation and discipline through regular check-ins and shared responsibilities.

IMPORTANCE OF AN ACCOUNTABILITY BUDDY

1. **Increased Motivation:** Having someone to share your progress with can greatly enhance your motivation. The desire not to let your buddy down can push you to take action even when your enthusiasm wanes.
2. **Objective Feedback**: An accountability buddy provides honest feedback, helping you see blind spots in your strategies. This objective perspective is invaluable for personal development and overcoming obstacles.
3. **Shared Knowledge and Resources:** Partners often bring different skills, knowledge, and resources to the table. Learning from each other's experiences and insights can accelerate progress and introduce new methods for achieving goals.
4. **Emotional Support:** The journey towards any significant goal can be emotionally taxing. An accountability buddy offers support during setbacks and celebrates your successes, making the journey less isolating.
5. **Consistency:** Regular check-ins ensure that you remain consistent in your efforts. This consistency is often the key to achieving long-term objectives.

Example: Studying for Professional Certification

Imagine two colleagues, Ana and Bob, who both aim to pass a challenging professional certification that will greatly advance their careers. They decide to become accountability partners, each committed to passing the exam within six months.

CHAPTER 3: STICK TO THE PLAN

- **Planning and Goal Setting:** They start by setting clear, measurable goals for their study timelines and decide on weekly milestones. Each Sunday, they plan their study schedule for the coming week, aligning their topics so they can discuss complex subjects together.
- **Regular Check-ins:** Ana and Bob agree to daily check-ins via a quick morning text sharing their main goal for the day and a brief evening call to discuss what they've accomplished. This routine keeps them both honest and on track.
- **Sharing Resources:** They share books, online resources, and interesting articles related to their certification topics. When Ana finds a particularly useful online forum, she introduces Bob to it, and they both benefit from the additional insights.
- **Overcoming Challenges:** When Bob struggles with a particular section of the material, Ana offers to help review the topic with him. During their review session, Ana uses her strengths in explaining concepts to help Bob grasp the material, enhancing both their understandings.
- **Celebrating Milestones:** Each time they complete a major section of their study material, Ana and Bob celebrate with a small reward, like a coffee out together. These celebrations keep morale high and provide something to look forward to.

At the end of six months, both Ana and Bob pass their certification exam. Their success is not just a product of their individual efforts but also the support, motivation, and accountability they provided to each other throughout the preparation process.

This example illustrates how an accountability buddy can transform a daunting task into a more manageable and enjoyable journey, ultimately leading to greater success and shared achievement.

PRACTICING SELF DISCIPLINE

Understanding Self-Discipline

Self-discipline can be understood as the ability to pursue what one thinks is right despite temptations to abandon it. It is often associated with being able to defer gratification, resist unhealthy excesses, and focus long term. But beyond these, self-discipline is crucial for setting and achieving personal and professional goals in a systematic and sustainable way.

THE BENEFITS OF SELF-DISCIPLINE

1. **Achievement of Goals:** Self-discipline is often the determining factor between achieving a goal or not. It fuels consistent work towards the completion of tasks and objectives, regardless of the desire to give up.
2. **Increased Self-Esteem:** As you meet your goals through disciplined actions, your self-esteem naturally increases. You begin to trust yourself more and feel confident in your ability to face new challenges.
3. **Stress Reduction:** People with a high degree of self-discipline experience less stress, as they are less prone to procrastinate and more likely to keep their commitments and manage their time effectively.
4. **Better Health:** Many aspects of health, from diet and exercise to sleep and stress management, are influenced by self-discipline. Practicing self-discipline in these areas can lead to better overall health and wellbeing.

HOW TO DEVELOP SELF-DISCIPLINE

1. **Set Clear Goals and Create a Plan:** Start by defining clear, achievable goals. Break these goals into small, manageable steps and set deadlines for each step to keep yourself accountable.

2. **Understand Your Weaknesses:** Self-awareness is crucial in self-discipline. Understand where your temptations lie and set up strategies to resist them. For example, if you struggle with procrastination on social media, use apps that limit your time on these platforms.

3. **Build Consistent Routines:** Routines can automate good behavior and reduce the mental effort needed to make disciplined choices. Establish daily routines that move you towards your goals.

4. **Practice Delayed Gratification:** Train yourself to wait for a better reward. You can practice this skill in small ways, like resisting the urge to check your phone immediately or saving money for a larger purchase instead of making impulse buys.

5. **Use Reminders and Accountability:** Keep your goals visible with reminders that can motivate you and keep you focused. Also, sharing your goals with a friend or a mentor can provide external accountability.

Example: A Fitness Journey

Consider someone aiming to improve their physical health by incorporating exercise into their daily routine. The journey begins with setting specific goals such as working out for 30 minutes a day, five days a week. To build self-discipline, they might start by scheduling workouts at the same time each day, making this new habit a part of their routine.

Over time, the initial resistance to exercise diminishes, and the routine becomes a normal part of their day. They resist the temptation to skip a workout by focusing on how good they will feel afterward and the progress they are making toward their health goals. By sticking to their plan regardless of mood or circumstances, they develop stronger self-discipline, which can then be applied to other areas of life, such as diet and work ethic.

Self-discipline is a powerful skill that can be developed through consistent practice and mindfulness. By understanding and implementing strategies to enhance self-discipline, you can improve not only your ability to achieve goals but also your overall quality of life.

DEVELOPING AND PRACTICING DETERMINATION

Determination is a powerful personal trait characterized by a steadfast commitment to achieving specific objectives despite obstacles and setbacks. It involves the mental toughness and perseverance needed to pursue a goal with unwavering focus. People who embody determination are often admired for their grit, a quality that enables them to push through difficulties and maintain their pursuit of success against all odds.

The Nature of Determination

At its core, determination is the inner strength that drives individuals to continue their efforts to reach their goals, regardless of the complexity of the challenges they face. It's about having a clear vision and not allowing distractions or discouragements to sway you from your path. Determination is not just about the strength to continue but also involves making calculated choices that align with long-term objectives.

THE BENEFITS OF BEING DETERMINED

1. **Achieving Goals:** Determination is crucial in transforming ambitions into achievements. The resolve to meet challenges head-on and work through them often leads to success where others might give up.
2. **Overcoming Failures:** Determination helps individuals to see failures as mere obstacles rather than endpoints. This resilience is critical in learning from mistakes and not being defeated by them.
3. **Inspiring Others:** Determined individuals often inspire those around them. Their commitment and success can motivate peers to adopt a similar mindset and approach to challenges.
4. **Personal Growth:** The journey of chasing a difficult goal builds character, skills, and self-awareness. Each challenge overcome is a step towards personal growth.
5. **Long-Term Satisfaction and Fulfillment:** Achieving goals through determination brings a sense of satisfaction and fulfillment that short-term successes seldom provide. It contributes to a lasting sense of accomplishment.

HOW TO CULTIVATE DETERMINATION

1. **Set Clear and Meaningful Goals:** Clearly defined goals that are deeply meaningful to the individual can fuel determination. Understanding why the goal is important can sustain motivation over the long haul.
2. **Develop a Plan:** Break down the goal into manageable steps. Planning helps in foreseeing potential challenges and equipping oneself with strategies to overcome them.

3. **Stay Focused:** Keep your ultimate goal in mind and regularly remind yourself of the bigger picture. Avoid distractions and stay mentally and physically focused on tasks that lead to the achievement of the goal.
4. **Build a Support Network:** Surround yourself with supportive people who encourage your efforts and believe in your ability to succeed. This can significantly enhance your resilience and determination.
5. **Embrace Challenges:** View challenges as opportunities to grow and prove your capabilities. This mindset shift can turn difficult situations into moments of triumph.

Example: Pursuing a Career Change

Consider the example of someone determined to shift careers from a corporate job to becoming a professional artist. This person might start by dedicating evenings to develop artistic skills, despite the initial lack of expertise and potential criticism. They might face financial uncertainty or skepticism from peers, but their determination would drive them to keep improving their craft.

By setting up small exhibitions, receiving feedback, and continuously learning, they steadily build a portfolio. Over time, their commitment leads to opportunities such as gallery representations or commercial projects, culminating in a successful career shift, inspired solely by their determination to follow a passion against the odds.

In summary, determination is an essential ingredient for success that, when coupled with a clear vision and strategic planning, can help overcome substantial barriers. It is the force that pushes individuals to rise after each fall and continue the journey towards their dreams, making it a universally respected and powerful trait to cultivate.

Persistence is the quality of continuing steadily despite problems or difficulties. It's a fundamental trait shared by many successful individuals across various fields, from entrepreneurs and scientists to artists and athletes. The essence of persistence lies in maintaining action against all odds, showing tenacity and steadfastness in following a course of action. This unyielding spirit is often what separates temporary failure from lasting success.

HOW PERSISTENCE PAYS OFF

Persistence pays off by turning challenges into opportunities and failures into lessons. Here are some key ways that persistence leads to success:

1. **Mastering Skills:** Skills in any field require time and repeated effort to develop. Whether it's playing a musical instrument, coding, or playing sports, persistent practice is essential for mastery. Each repetition refines technique and deepens understanding.
2. **Overcoming Obstacles:** Persistent individuals are more likely to devise creative solutions to overcome obstacles because they are committed to reaching their goals. They don't back down when faced with setbacks; instead, they learn and adapt.
3. **Achieving Long-Term Goals:** Many goals, such as earning a degree, building a business, or writing a book, require sustained effort. Persistence ensures that one continues to make progress towards these goals, regardless of how distant they may seem.
4. **Building Confidence:** Each small victory achieved through persistence builds self-confidence. Over time, this confidence reinforces a person's belief in their ability to succeed, fueling further efforts and fostering a positive cycle of growth and achievement.

5. **Gaining Credibility and Trust:** People who consistently demonstrate persistence earn the trust and respect of their peers and superiors. This credibility can open doors to new opportunities and collaborations.

CULTIVATING PERSISTENCE

Persistence can be cultivated through various practical steps. They include:

- **Set Clear Goals:** Clearly defined goals provide direction and a measure of progress. They keep you focused and purposeful.
- **Develop a Routine:** Consistency in action can be achieved through a structured routine or habits that support your goals.
- **Stay Motivated:** Keep your motivation alive by reminding yourself of the importance of your goals. Visualizing the outcomes can help maintain focus.
- **Learn from Setbacks:** Instead of getting discouraged by failures, analyze them to understand what went wrong and how you can avoid similar mistakes in the future.
- **Seek Support:** Sometimes, persistence can be bolstered by the encouragement of others. Support from mentors, peers, or family can provide the necessary push to keep going.

Example: The Story of a Startup

Consider the story of a tech startup aiming to revolutionize the way people interact with their homes through smart technology. The initial concept might fail to attract investors, and the prototype could be fraught with bugs. Through persistent efforts, the team refines the technology, learns from each round of feedback, and gradually improves their pitch.

Despite numerous rejections, they continue to improve and adapt their product. Their persistence pays off when a major tech conference allows them a platform to showcase their improved prototype, leading to interest from venture capitalists. This initial breakthrough, hard-earned through persistent effort, could eventually lead to success in a competitive market.

Having an accountability buddy, practicing self-discipline, determination, and persistence are invaluable assets in sticking to a plan and achieving our goals. Together, these qualities form a powerful combination that propels us forward on our journey toward achieving our goals. With an accountability buddy by our side, we stay accountable and motivated. With self-discipline, we stay focused and on track. With determination, we overcome challenges and obstacles. And with persistence, we keep pushing forward until we reach our destination.

As we embrace these qualities and incorporate them into our daily lives, we empower ourselves to stick to our plans, overcome obstacles, and achieve our greatest aspirations. With accountability, discipline, determination, and persistence as our allies, there is no limit to what we can accomplish.

Chapter 4
BE GRATEFUL

The Power of Gratitude in Daily Life

The stories I have chosen to share in this chapter continue to hold a special place in my heart, even to this day. As I have previously mentioned, my upbringing during my younger years, particularly my time in elementary school, was what one might consider middle class. Despite not having an abundance of material possessions, my mother worked diligently to provide for our family, while my father, despite my parents' divorce when I was just two years old, remained an active presence in my life. He gifted us with luxuries such as a washing machine, a color TV, and new furniture for our living and dining rooms—early perks that were not common in every household in Mexico back in the late 1970s.

Despite the challenges of divorce, my parents maintained a strong friendship and always prioritized my well-being. While I lived with my mother full-time, my father made a point to spend quality time with me every Wednesday afternoon and every other Sunday. Looking back, I realize how fortunate I was to have such dedicated and loving parents. Despite the limited time we had together, my father made sure our time was meaningful and memorable. He planned outings to the movies, parks, pet stores, and visits to my grandmother, always armed with stories and jokes to share. Inadvertently, my parents instilled in me a profound sense of security, for which I am eternally grateful. The opportunity to spend quality time with both parents during my upbringing imbued me with a deep appreciation for familial bonds and the importance of nurturing relationships.

Attending a private bilingual elementary school provided me with numerous opportunities for personal and academic growth. I engaged in extracurricular activities such as dance, English, and drama, which enriched my educational experience and fostered my creativity. However, as I entered my teenage years, my life underwent significant changes. My mother's decision to move to a new city, her decision to send me abroad to my aunt's house, and the arrival of my baby sister would profoundly impact the dynamics of our family and shape my adolescent experiences. Yet, amidst the changes and challenges, I remained grounded in gratitude for the love and support bestowed upon me by my family.

Despite the challenges and changes that came my way, the foundation of love, support, and security laid by my parents during my formative years continued to guide me through life's ups and downs. Their unwavering commitment to my happiness and well-being set the stage for resilience and gratitude, qualities that would serve me well as I navigated the complexities of adolescence and beyond.

In essence, the stories recounted in this chapter serve as a testament to the enduring power of gratitude—a virtue that permeates every aspect of my life, guiding me through moments of joy and adversity alike.

Story No. 1: Navigating Adversity with Optimism

At the tender age of thirteen, I embarked on a journey that would shape my resilience and optimism in the face of adversity. Moving to Pasadena, California, with my beloved aunt and uncle to improve my English and delve into American history was both daunting and exhilarating. Yet, amidst the whirlwind of change, I encountered challenges that tested my tenacity.

Placed in ESL classes alongside students from diverse backgrounds, I found myself navigating unfamiliar territories. Despite feeling different from the majority, I refused to succumb to the limitations of ESL education. Determined to fully immerse myself in English, I took a bold step and requested a transfer to regular English classes, despite the inevitable struggles that accompanied this decision. Armed with nothing but determination and a trusty English-Spanish dictionary, I embarked on a journey of academic and personal growth.

Throughout that school year and the following one, I persevered, earning accolades in honors classes and forming meaningful connections with peers from various cultural backgrounds. Embracing the role of a leader within our multicultural cohort, I honed my leadership skills and developed a newfound sense of discipline and focus.

The eighteen-month period in Pasadena proved to be a pivotal chapter in my life, instilling in me the resilience to navigate change and embrace new experiences. Over the years, as I traversed six cities across Mexico, the United States, and Canada, my ability to adapt and thrive in diverse environments became second nature. Each move presented its own set of challenges, yet I approached them with a sense of optimism and gratitude.

Amidst the uncertainty of when I would reunite with my mother, I found comfort in daily rituals that reinforced my optimism. Every morning, during my walk to school, I paused to express gratitude for the blessings of the previous day—the moments of joy and learning at school, the warmth of my aunt's home, and the cherished traits of my mother. With each step, I affirmed my belief in the universe's plan for my return home, drawing strength from the power of gratitude and positivity.

In retrospect, those moments of reflection and gratitude during my morning walks served as anchors of hope and resilience, guiding me through the challenges of adolescence with unwavering optimism. They were a testament to the transformative power of gratitude, reminding me that even in the face of uncertainty, there is always something to be thankful for.

Story No. 2: Stranded Without Fuel

Upon my return to Tijuana, Mexico, from Pasadena, California, my life took on a new set of challenges. Situated on the northern border of Mexico with the United States, Tijuana was a bustling city where thousands crossed the border daily to attend school or work in San Diego, just a stone's throw away. At the age of seventeen, I went with my mother to a used car dealership, striking a deal for my very first car—a sleek black 1984 Dodge Charger. With the keys to my newfound freedom came a wave of responsibility: monthly payments, gas, insurance, and all my school expenses were now my burden to bear.

In the landscape of 1988, where the minimum wage in California was a mere $4.25 per hour, every penny counted. I carefully balanced my budget and accounted for each expense. Yet, despite my diligence, there were moments when unexpected costs threatened to disrupt my precarious financial equilibrium.

One such day stands out vividly in my memory. With less than twenty dollars in my bank account and a near-empty gas tank, I embarked on my daily commute across the border, knowing that I had just enough to reach my destination but unsure of how I would return home. The possibility of uncertainty appeared large, but instead of succumbing to fear, I chose to embrace gratitude.

Throughout the day, as I navigated through work and classes, I made a conscious effort to express gratitude for every aspect of my life. With each step from my office to my car in the parking lot, I offered thanks to the universe for the blessings of mobility and opportunity. Though the fear threatened to overwhelm me, I held onto a sense of gratitude, trusting that somehow, everything would fall into place.

As fate would have it, a turn of events unfolded at the local post office—a place I frequented to check our family's post office box. Nestled within a legal-size envelope was a surprise that defied all expectations, cash from my father, sent as a contribution towards an immigration form he needed me to submit on his behalf. In that moment, a rush of emotions flooded over me—surprise, relief, gratitude. It was as if the universe had conspired to affirm my faith, delivering a timely reminder that even in moments of uncertainty, there is always something to be grateful for.

That day, as I filled up my gas tank with newfound abundance, I was reminded of the transformative power of gratitude. It was a lesson engraved into my consciousness—a beacon of hope that guided me through future challenges yet to come.

Story No. 3: An Extended Stay in Canada

In the spring leading up to my nineteenth birthday, an unexpected opportunity knocked at my door: my aunt Rosario, who had relocated to Canada several years earlier, extended an invitation for me to experience life in Canada. While this chapter delves into the theme of gratitude, it's crucial to underscore the importance of taking decisive action. Every dream requires proactive steps to transform into reality.

As I navigated through the complexities of educational pursuits, car ownership, and contributions to my mom, my responsibilities weighed heavily upon me. My mother had recently purchased a new home, and I had committed to assisting her with the monthly mortgage payments amidst the financial strain of my younger sister's daycare expenses. When my aunt Rosario reached out to me, excitement coursed through my veins; this would mark my inaugural venture into living abroad outside Mexico and the United States, a chance to spend the vibrant months of spring and summer immersed

CHAPTER 4: BE GRATEFUL

in a foreign culture.

In those pre-digital days, planning such a trip required countless visits to the library, poring over books and magazines for information. The process began in December of the previous year, as I meticulously crafted my itinerary. I shared my plans with both my manager and the owner of the insurance agency where I worked, ensuring transparency and accountability.

Navigating the intricacies of international travel, I secured health insurance and booked my plane ticket, with my aunt generously covering all expenses. Gratitude permeated every aspect of my preparations; I penned heartfelt letters to my aunt, expressing profound appreciation for her unwavering support, knowing full well that without her assistance, the trip would have remained a distant dream.

Despite the excitement of the impending adventure, I remained cognizant of my financial obligations back home. Determined to honor my commitments, I resolved to earn enough in Canada to fulfill my car and home payments. As the departure date drew nearer, I bid farewell to my colleagues with a tinge of sadness, grateful for their understanding and support.

The Canadian summer unfolded as a kaleidoscope of unforgettable experiences. From the thundering majesty of Niagara Falls to the cultural richness of Ottawa, Toronto, and Montreal, every moment was steeped in gratitude. Managing the vibrant staff at my aunt's lemonade stands provided invaluable leadership opportunities, while leisurely walks, invigorating hikes, and serene boat rides by the lake filled my days with joy.

As the season waned and thoughts turned homeward, I compiled a catalog of gratitude, documenting the myriad blessings and cherished memories. With anticipation tinged with optimism, I embarked on my journey back to the United

States, confident that new horizons awaited me.

True to my belief, opportunity knocked swiftly upon my return. In less than two weeks, I secured a new job that not only aligned with my aspirations but also offered a welcomed financial boost. It was as if my optimism had unlocked the door to better opportunities.

Reflecting on this transformative experience, I am filled with comfort and gratitude. My aunt Rosario, whose untimely passing from leukemia at the age of 48 robbed us of future moments together, remains forever cherished in my memories. Her generosity and the adventures we shared in Canada are imprinted permanently in my heart. Thank you, Tia Rosario, for the gift of unforgettable moments and lasting inspiration.

How is Gratitude Practiced?

Remember that practicing gratitude is a personal journey, and what works best for one person may not be the same for another. Experiment with different methods and find what resonates most with you. The key is to cultivate a mindset of appreciation and recognize the abundance that surrounds you, even in the midst of life's challenges.

1. **Gratitude Journaling:** Set aside a few minutes each day to write down things on why you are grateful. Reflect on moments of joy, acts of kindness, or even small blessings like a sunny day or a good meal.
2. **Morning Gratitude:** Start your day by expressing gratitude for the opportunities and blessings that lie ahead. Take a moment to appreciate the new day and set a positive tone for the hours ahead.
3. **Express Thanks:** Make a conscious effort to thank others for their kindness, support, or contributions. Whether it's a verbal "thank you," a handwritten note, or a simple text

message, expressing gratitude strengthens relationships and spreads positivity.

4. **Mindful Appreciation:** Practice mindfulness by fully immersing yourself in the present moment and appreciating the beauty around you. Notice the sights, sounds, and sensations that bring you joy and express gratitude for them.

5. **Reflect on Challenges:** Instead of dwelling on setbacks or difficulties, reframe them as opportunities for growth. Reflect on the lessons learned from challenging experiences and express gratitude for the strength and resilience they have cultivated within you.

6. **Gratitude Walks:** Take a walk outdoors and focus on the beauty of nature around you. As you walk, consciously acknowledge and appreciate the sights, sounds, and smells of the natural world, expressing gratitude for the wonders of the environment.

7. **Gratitude Rituals:** Create rituals or routines that incorporate expressions of gratitude, such as saying grace before meals, sharing gratitude at family gatherings, or ending the day with a reflection on moments of appreciation.

8. **Acts of Kindness:** Pay it forward by performing acts of kindness for others. Whether it's offering a helping hand, lending a listening ear, or performing random acts of kindness, spreading positivity can cultivate gratitude in both yourself and others.

9. **Gratitude Meditation:** Practice guided meditation focused on gratitude, where you visualize and reflect on the things you are thankful for. This can help cultivate a sense of inner peace and appreciation.

10. **Gratitude Challenges:** Challenge yourself to find

something to be grateful for each day, even on challenging days. This can help shift your perspective and cultivate a habit of gratitude over time.

Start a 21-Day Gratitude Challenge Plan

Week 1: Self-Reflection and Appreciation

- **Day 1:** Write down three things you are grateful for about yourself.
- **Day 2:** Reflect on a recent experience that made you happy.
- **Day 3:** Send a thank-you note or message to someone who has helped you.
- **Day 4:** Take a moment to appreciate your home and the comfort it provides.
- **Day 5:** Acknowledge the work you do (whether paid or unpaid) and its impact.
- **Day 6:** Choose an object you use daily and reflect on how it makes your life easier.
- **Day 7:** Think about your body and the health you have; appreciate what it allows you to do.

Week 2: Expanding Gratitude Outward

- **Day 8:** Write about a friend and what you are grateful for about them.
- **Day 9:** Call or meet a family member and tell them why you appreciate them.
- **Day 10:** Observe nature; be thankful for the environment around you.
- **Day 11:** Express gratitude for your community (online or physical).

- **Day 12:** Appreciate something new you learned this week.
- **Day 13:** Recognize someone's effort or kindness without them knowing.
- **Day 14:** Donate to a cause you believe in and reflect on your ability to help others.

Week 3: Cultivating a Lifestyle of Gratitude

- **Day 15:** Write a positive review for a local business or service.
- **Day 16:** Find beauty in a piece of art or music and reflect on its impact on you.
- **Day 17:** Recognize an aspect of your daily routine you usually take for granted.
- **Day 18:** Write down a difficult experience and what it taught you.
- **Day 19:** Identify a mistake and appreciate the growth it brought.
- **Day 20:** Think about your past week and write down the best moment.
- **Day 21:** Plan a small celebration to mark the end of your gratitude challenge.

Tips for Success

- **Journaling:** Keep a gratitude journal where you can elaborate on your thoughts for each day.
- **Consistency:** Try to perform your gratitude practice at the same time each day to establish a routine.
- **Reflection:** Spend a few minutes each day reflecting on why you feel grateful for the day's prompt.

- **Sharing:** Consider sharing your daily gratitude with a friend or on social media to inspire others and enhance your experience.

This challenge can be the beginning of a lifelong practice that shifts your focus from what's missing in your life to the abundance that is already present. Enjoy your journey towards a more grateful and fulfilling life!

PRACTICE OPTIMISM

The science of optimism explores the psychological, physiological, and social benefits of maintaining a positive outlook on life. Optimism is more than just wishful thinking or blind positivity; it involves a mindset characterized by hopeful expectations and a belief that positive outcomes are possible, even in the face of adversity. Research in psychology, neuroscience, and medicine has revealed numerous benefits associated with optimism, ranging from improved mental health and well-being to better physical health outcomes and resilience in the face of challenges.

Psychological Benefits of Optimism

1. **Enhanced Mental Health:** Optimistic individuals tend to experience lower levels of stress, anxiety, and depression. They are better able to cope with setbacks and bounce back from adversity, leading to greater overall psychological well-being.
2. **Increased Happiness:** Optimism is strongly associated with feelings of happiness and life satisfaction. Optimistic individuals are more likely to experience positive emotions and have a greater sense of purpose and meaning in life.

3. **Improved Coping Skills:** Optimistic people tend to employ adaptive coping strategies when faced with challenges, such as seeking social support, reframing negative events in a positive light, and focusing on solutions rather than dwelling on problems.

Physiological Benefits of Optimism

1. **Better Physical Health:** Optimism is linked to a range of positive health outcomes, including lower blood pressure, reduced risk of cardiovascular disease, and improved immune function. Optimistic individuals are also more likely to engage in health-promoting behaviors such as exercise, healthy eating, and regular medical check-ups.

2. **Faster Recovery:** Optimistic individuals tend to recover more quickly from illness, surgery, or injury compared to their pessimistic counterparts. A positive outlook can boost the body's natural healing processes and enhance resilience in the face of physical challenges.

Social Benefits of Optimism

1. **Stronger Relationships:** Optimistic individuals tend to have larger social networks and stronger social support systems. They are more likely to build and maintain positive relationships with others, which can provide a buffer against stress and promote overall well-being.

2. **Leadership and Success:** Optimistic leaders are often more effective in motivating and inspiring others, fostering a positive work environment, and achieving success in their endeavors. Their optimistic outlook can be contagious, inspiring confidence, and perseverance in those around them.

Cultivating Optimism

While some individuals may naturally possess a more optimistic outlook, optimism is also a skill that can be cultivated and strengthened over time. Strategies for fostering optimism include:

1. **Practicing Gratitude:** Regularly expressing gratitude for the positive aspects of life can help shift focus away from negativity and cultivate a more optimistic mindset.
2. **Challenging Negative Thoughts:** Recognizing and challenging negative self-talk and cognitive distortions can help reframe situations in a more positive light.
3. **Setting Realistic Goals:** Setting achievable goals and celebrating small victories along the way can boost confidence and reinforce optimism.
4. **Cultivating Positive Relationships:** Surrounding oneself with supportive, positive people can help nurture an optimistic outlook and provide encouragement during challenging times.

Incorporating gratitude, optimism, and a selective approach to thankfulness into our daily practices can have a profound impact on our ability to achieve our goals. By fostering a positive mindset, maintaining hope and resilience, and focusing our efforts on what truly matters, we create a strong foundation for success and fulfillment in all areas of our lives. As we continue on our journey, let us embrace these practices wholeheartedly and harness their transformative power to create the life we envision.

Chapter 5
LIFT OTHERS

The Impact of Rising Together

As I shared in the first chapter, at twenty-two years old, I found myself immersed in this coastal paradise as my husband pursued his dream of becoming a physician.

Thus, I embarked on a new path, embracing the role of an ESL teacher for the local elementary school children and helping my husband with vaccinations and administrative work. This experience solidified my conviction that my true purpose lay in serving others and facilitating their success. This pivotal experience in Zipolite marked the genesis of my journey toward servant leadership—a philosophy centered on paying it forward, mentoring, and uplifting those around me.

As I reflect on my journey and share my story with others, I emphasize the importance of this powerful **fifth step** in my personal roadmap to success: the commitment to lifting others. For in the act of serving and guiding, we not only shape our own destiny but also sow the seeds of a brighter, more compassionate future for all.

Servant leadership is like a multifaceted gem, reflecting different facets of care and empowerment depending on who you ask. For me, being a servant leader means more than just guiding from the front; it means sharing knowledge, fostering growth, and helping individuals unlock their full potential. It's about learning from those around you and working tirelessly to bring out the best in them. In my twenty-five-year career in the insurance industry, this philosophy has been my guiding light.

After bidding farewell to the shores of Zipolite, my husband and I embarked on a journey that led us to Mexico City and eventually to Pasadena, California. Along the way, I pursued certification in teaching ESL, a skill I put to use by volunteering as an ESL teacher and citizenship instructor. Serving my community became a cornerstone of my existence. The reciprocity of support reached its peak when my former students cheered me on at my own graduation, a touching reminder of the ripple effect of service and mentorship.

As I reflect on my journey, I realize that one of the most powerful steps in achieving success is the act of giving back. Whether through teaching, mentoring, volunteering, or facilitating workshops, the opportunity to uplift others is a privilege I hold dear. This ethos of service extends beyond my professional endeavors; it's a fundamental aspect of who I am.

Within the corporate realm, **mentoring** has been one of my greatest accomplishments. As a woman in insurance and the financial industry, a minority, and a Latina with roots in both Mexico and California, I've often found myself in a position to offer guidance and support to aspiring professionals. Through mentorship, I've discovered the immense value of empowering individuals to recognize their own strengths and capabilities. Instead of dictating a path, mentoring as a servant leader is about illuminating the potential within each person, often by providing an objective perspective that helps them see their own worth.

One of the most fulfilling aspects of mentorship is witnessing the transformation it ignites. I recall a mentee who approached me during an international event, seeking guidance and support.

It all started during an international event I organized, where CEOs from Brazil and Poland were featured speakers. One attendee, also from Brazil, approached me with excitement but hesitated to engage with the CEO. Sensing her apprehension, I introduced her to the CEO and facilitated a connection. This act of kindness led her to seek me out as her mentor.

During our initial meeting, I asked about her goals and aspirations to ensure a good fit for our mentorship. Recognizing her potential, I offered her a challenging opportunity to lead the rebranding of our Business Resource Group. Over the next six months, she spearheaded the initiative, conducting focus groups, and collaborating with marketing and design teams to create a new logo. Her confidence soared as she took on leadership roles and showcased her skills.

Together, we planned the launch of the rebranded initiative, which was met with enthusiasm and engagement from our organization. Our mentor-mentee relationship was built on honesty and trust, allowing her to open up about past obstacles hindering her growth. Her journey of success and resilience was featured in business magazines, and she even shared our story in a social media post, acknowledging the role I played in her development.

This experience exemplifies the impact of mentorship and the power of lifting others up. It's a reminder that anyone can be a mentor in their field and make a difference in someone's life. As we support and empower each other, we create a ripple effect of growth and success throughout our communities.

As I share my experiences, I encourage others to embrace the role of mentorship in their own journeys. Whether it's offering guidance to a colleague, lending a listening ear to a friend, or providing opportunities for growth and development, the impact of lifting others reverberates far beyond the individual. Together, we can create a culture of support and empowerment, where success is measured not only by personal achievements but by the lives we touch and the legacies we leave behind.

Throughout my career, I've been passionate about fostering diversity and inclusion within the companies I have worked for. As I shared before, in 2020 with the resounding success of our initial class, elevink came into being. I count myself fortunate to have had my sister as a supporter, generously extending her time, expertise and network. In addition, as the business plan evolved, I recruited a partner-in-crime to collaborate with, aiding in content creation and workshop facilitation. Interestingly, she had once been my mentee, and her journey is worth sharing.

It all started when I received a networking request on a popular global platform. Intrigued by her local proximity in New Jersey and our shared background in insurance, I accepted her invitation. Shortly after, she expressed admiration for my career trajectory and sought mentorship. I believe in understanding the mentee's needs thoroughly, so we engaged in an exploratory conversation. I made it clear that while I could offer guidance and support, the mentee ultimately drives their own success through commitment and internal work. Transparency is key in mentorship dynamics.

Our first meeting in person was promising. Armed with a list of questions, she demonstrated her dedication. We agreed to embark on a mentor-mentee relationship. However, our plans were swiftly altered by the onset of the pandemic in March 2020, forcing us into virtual sessions for the next eighteen months.

Despite the challenges, our collaboration thrived. I invited her to join elevink activities, and together we led cohort meetings and weekend boot camps. With a commitment to inclusivity, we kept opportunities virtual, attracting participants from across the country. Our impact expanded, touching the lives of over three hundred individuals through various initiatives, including our monthly podcast, *elevink Connect*, designed to inspire professionals and ignite career advancement.

Feedback from participants has been overwhelmingly positive, with many citing personal growth and tangible career outcomes. Graduation ceremonies are poignant, filled with hope and camaraderie. Notably, our follow-up surveys revealed that nearly half of the graduates experienced promotions, job changes, or career advancements after completing the program.

As for my mentee and other elevink graduates, their stories of success were recently celebrated in the Hispanic Star's anthology, *Hispanic Stars Rising: The New Face of Power*. I take pride in being able to recognize their achievements in this manner and remain committed to opening doors for others, ensuring that opportunities for growth and empowerment are accessible to all.

Even today, my dedication to serving and leading my community remains unwavering, particularly in the realm of diversity and equality. I had the honor of being one of the twenty-five individuals on the national founding alliance for Hispanic Star, a dynamic platform aimed at propelling Hispanics in the United States to become significant contributors to economic growth and cultural evolution. Witnessing its growth into regional hubs across the country has been immensely gratifying.

In 2021, I seized the opportunity to mobilize alumni from elevink to support a noble cause during Hispanic Heritage month. Together, we volunteered with the Feed Our Starving Children program, providing nourishment to those in need. It was a heartwarming experience, aligning perfectly with my commitment to serving the broader community.

Reflecting on past endeavors, I recall my involvement during the 2000 United States Census, where I actively engaged in door-to-door outreach to gather vital information from Hispanic communities. Our goal was simple yet crucial—to ensure every family was accounted for in government data, thereby influencing decisions on various social issues. As a servant leader, it was my way of uplifting the community indirectly through the census.

Furthermore, my involvement with Hispanics Inspiring Students' Performance and Achievement (HISPA) in both New Jersey and Florida has been deeply fulfilling. This initiative seeks role models to inspire students through school presentations. Drawing from my own experiences, I've been actively involved in school activities, sharing insights into Mexican traditions and fostering collaboration between Mexico and America. Being recognized as the 2018 HISPA Champion of the Year was a humbling acknowledgment of my efforts.

In 2016, I took another step towards empowering youth by founding the Univerbond Camp. Through interactive workshops, this program aimed to inspire children, teens, and women to pursue their dreams using my *Five Keys to Success*. Witnessing their growth and enthusiasm has been incredibly rewarding.

For me, servant leadership isn't just a title or a one-time act, it's a way of life rooted in my core values. It's about consistently lifting others as I rise myself, earning trust and respect through genuine care and support. When you live authentically as a servant leader, both individuals and communities recognize and appreciate your impact, making it a deeply fulfilling journey.

Here are the practical applications of the concepts of how you too can lift others by volunteering, mentoring or becoming a servant leader:

Mentoring

Becoming a mentor is a rewarding experience that allows you to make a positive impact on someone's life while also fostering personal growth and development. Here are some steps to guide you through the process of becoming a mentor:

1. **Reflect on Your Experiences and Skills:** Take some time to reflect on your own life experiences, both personal and professional. Identify the skills, knowledge, and expertise you have acquired throughout your journey that you can share with others. Consider what areas you excel in and where you can offer valuable guidance and support.

2. **Define Your Mentoring Goals:** Clarify your objectives and what you hope to achieve as a mentor. Think about the specific areas or topics you want to focus on, whether it's career development, personal growth, academic success, or a combination of these. Having clear goals will help you tailor your mentoring approach to meet the needs of your mentee.

3. **Identify Potential Mentees:** Look for individuals who could benefit from your guidance and support. This could be someone within your professional network, a colleague, a student, or even a friend or family member. Consider reaching out to organizations or programs that facilitate mentoring relationships, such as local schools, universities, or community groups.

4. **Initiate Contact:** Once you've identified potential mentees, take the initiative to reach out and express your interest in mentoring them. Start by introducing yourself and explaining why you believe you can be a valuable mentor to them. Be genuine and sincere in your approach, and emphasize your willingness to support and guide them in achieving their goals.

5. **Establish Mutual Expectations:** Set clear expectations for the mentoring relationship from the outset. Discuss what both you and your mentee hope to gain from the experience, as well as the frequency and format of your interactions. Establishing open communication and mutual respect is essential for a successful mentoring partnership.

6. **Build Trust and Rapport:** Invest time and effort in building a strong relationship with your mentee based on trust, respect, and rapport. Listen actively to their concerns, interests, and aspirations, and offer constructive feedback and encouragement. Be patient, empathetic, and supportive as they navigate challenges and pursue their goals.

7. **Provide Guidance and Support:** As a mentor, your role is to provide guidance, support, and encouragement to your mentee as they work towards their objectives. Share your knowledge, expertise, and insights, and offer practical advice and resources to help them overcome obstacles and make informed decisions. Be a sounding board for their ideas and concerns, and help them develop critical thinking and problem-solving skills.

8. **Encourage Reflection and Growth:** Encourage your mentee to reflect on their experiences, set goals, and take proactive steps towards personal and professional growth. Help them identify their strengths and areas for improvement, and empower them to take ownership of their development journey. Celebrate their achievements and milestones along the way, and continue to offer guidance and support as needed.

9. **Maintain Regular Communication:** Stay engaged and connected with your mentee through regular communication and check-ins. Schedule regular meetings or touchpoints to discuss progress, address challenges, and provide ongoing support and guidance. Be accessible and responsive to their needs, and be flexible in adapting to their changing circumstances.

10. **Evaluate and Adapt:** Periodically evaluate the effectiveness of your mentoring relationship and make adjustments as needed. Solicit feedback from your mentee on their experience and what they find helpful

or beneficial. Be open to constructive criticism and suggestions for improvement, and continue to refine your approach to better meet the needs of your mentee.

By following these steps and embracing the role of mentorship with enthusiasm and dedication, you can make a meaningful difference in the lives of others while also enriching your own personal and professional journey.

Volunteerism

Selecting a volunteer opportunity that aligns with your interests, skills, and values is key to making a meaningful contribution to your community while also fulfilling your personal goals. Here are some steps to guide you through the process of selecting a volunteer opportunity:

1. **Reflect on Your Passions and Interests:** Start by reflecting on your passions, interests, and causes that are meaningful to you. Consider the issues or areas of need that you feel strongly about, whether it's education, environmental conservation, social justice, animal welfare, or something else entirely.

2. **Identify Your Skills and Strengths:** Assess your skills, talents, and strengths that you can contribute to a volunteer role. Think about what you excel at, whether it's communication, organization, teaching, writing, or hands-on activities. Identifying your strengths will help you find opportunities where you can make the greatest impact.

3. **Consider Your Availability:** Take into account your availability and schedule when selecting a volunteer opportunity. Determine how much time you can realistically commit to volunteering each week or month, whether it's a few hours, a full day, or ongoing long-term

involvement. Choose opportunities that fit within your schedule and allow you to maintain a healthy balance with other commitments.

4. **Research Volunteer Opportunities:** Once you have a sense of your interests, skills, and availability, research volunteer opportunities that align with your criteria. Explore local nonprofit organizations, community groups, schools, churches, and online platforms that connect volunteers with opportunities. Consider reaching out directly to organizations or attending volunteer fairs or events to learn more about available roles.

5. **Evaluate the Organization and Cause:** Before committing to a volunteer opportunity, take the time to evaluate the organization and the cause they support. Research the organization's mission, values, and reputation, and ensure that they are aligned with your own beliefs and principles. Consider factors such as the organization's impact, transparency, and accountability.

6. **Assess the Volunteer Role:** Review the specific volunteer roles and responsibilities associated with each opportunity you're considering. Consider whether the role matches your skills, interests, and goals, and whether it provides opportunities for personal growth and learning. Clarify expectations around time commitment, training, supervision, and support.

7. **Connect with the Organization:** Reach out to the organization or volunteer coordinator to express your interest and inquire about available opportunities. Ask questions to gain a better understanding of the volunteer role, the organization's needs, and how your skills and interests can contribute to their mission. Request information about any required training, background checks, or other prerequisites for volunteering.

8. **Seek Feedback and Recommendations:** If possible, seek feedback and recommendations from current or former volunteers who have experience with the organization or opportunity you're considering. They can provide valuable insights into the volunteer experience, the organization's culture, and the impact of their work.

9. **Attend an Orientation or Trial Period:** If offered, attend an orientation session or participate in a trial period to get a feel for the volunteer opportunity and the organization's culture. Use this time to ask questions, meet other volunteers and staff members, and assess whether the opportunity is the right fit for you.

10. **Make an Informed Decision:** Based on your research, evaluation, and personal preferences, make an informed decision about which volunteer opportunity to pursue. Choose an opportunity that resonates with you personally and where you believe you can make a meaningful contribution. Remember that volunteering is a two-way street, and finding the right fit benefits both you and the organization you support.

By following these steps and taking the time to carefully evaluate your options, you can find a volunteer opportunity that aligns with your interests, values, and goals, allowing you to make a positive impact in your community and beyond.

Servant Leadership

Becoming a servant leader is a journey of personal growth and development focused on serving others and empowering those around you. Here are some steps you can take to embrace servant leadership:

1. **Understand the Principles of Servant Leadership:** Familiarize yourself with the core principles of servant leadership, which include putting the needs of others first, empowering and developing people, fostering collaboration, and serving as a humble steward of resources. Study the works of renowned servant leaders like Robert K. Greenleaf and explore how their ideas can be applied in your own life and leadership practices.

2. **Cultivate Empathy and Compassion:** Develop empathy and compassion for others by seeking to understand their perspectives, experiences, and needs. Practice active listening and engage in meaningful conversations to connect with people on a deeper level. Show genuine concern for the well-being of others and strive to make a positive difference in their lives.

3. **Lead by Example:** Lead by example and demonstrate servant leadership behaviors in your everyday actions and interactions. Show humility, integrity, and authenticity in your words and deeds. Be willing to roll up your sleeves and pitch in alongside others, rather than simply delegating tasks from a distance.

4. **Serve Others Selflessly:** Look for opportunities to serve others selflessly, both within and outside of your formal leadership role. Offer your time, expertise, and resources to support the needs of individuals, teams, and communities. Focus on how you can contribute to the growth, development, and success of others without expecting anything in return.

5. **Empower and Develop Others:** Empower and develop the people around you by providing them with opportunities for growth, learning, and advancement. Encourage autonomy, creativity, and initiative, and provide support and guidance as needed. Invest in mentorship, coaching, and training programs to help others reach their full potential.

6. **Build Relationships Based on Trust and Respect:** Build strong relationships with those you lead and serve based on trust, respect, and mutual understanding. Foster a culture of openness, collaboration, and inclusivity where everyone feels valued and heard. Create a supportive environment where people feel safe to express themselves, take risks, and learn from their mistakes.

7. **Lead with Purpose and Vision:** Lead with a clear sense of purpose and vision that inspires and motivates others to join you in your efforts. Communicate your vision with clarity and passion, and enlist others in co-creating shared goals and objectives. Align your actions and decisions with your values and vision, and seek to make a positive impact on the world around you.

8. **Continuously Learn and Grow:** Commit to continuous learning and growth as a servant leader. Seek feedback from others and be open to constructive criticism and self-reflection. Take advantage of opportunities for personal and professional development, such as workshops, courses, and networking events, to expand your skills and knowledge.

9. **Practice Gratitude and Generosity:** Practice gratitude and generosity in your leadership approach by recognizing and appreciating the contributions of others. Express thanks and praise for their efforts and achievements, and celebrate their successes. Be generous with your time, support, and resources, and look for ways to give back to your community and those in need.

10. **Inspire Others to Lead:** Inspire and empower others to embrace servant leadership and become leaders in their own right. Encourage them to develop their own leadership skills and qualities, and provide opportunities for them to take on leadership roles and responsibilities.

CHAPTER 5: LIFT OTHERS

Nurture a culture of leadership development and succession planning to ensure a legacy of servant leadership for future generations.

By embodying these principles and practices of servant leadership, you can make a positive difference in the lives of others and create a more compassionate, collaborative, and impactful world.

Mentoring, volunteerism, and servant leadership are powerful tools for elevating others and creating positive change in our communities and beyond. Through mentoring, we have the opportunity to guide and support individuals on their personal and professional journeys, helping them unlock their potential and achieve their goals. By sharing our knowledge, experiences, and insights, we can empower others to overcome challenges, seize opportunities, and realize their dreams.

Volunteerism allows us to give back to our communities and make a meaningful difference in the lives of others. By donating our time, skills, and resources, we can address pressing social issues, support vulnerable populations, and contribute to the common good. Whether it's serving meals at a homeless shelter, tutoring students in need, or participating in environmental clean-up efforts, every act of volunteerism has the power to uplift and inspire those we serve.

Servant leadership embodies the principles of humility, compassion, and selflessness, placing the needs of others above our own. By leading with empathy, integrity, and a genuine desire to serve, we can create environments where individuals feel valued, empowered, and supported. Through our actions and example, we can inspire others to become servant leaders themselves, multiplying the impact of our efforts and fostering a culture of kindness, collaboration, and collective achievement.

Together, mentoring, volunteerism, and servant leadership form a powerful trifecta of service and empowerment, enabling us to lift others up, nurture their potential, and create a more just, equitable, and compassionate world for all. As we continue on our journey of personal and professional growth, let us remain committed to serving others, lifting as we climb, and leaving a legacy of positive impact that extends far beyond ourselves.

- **What action are you now motivated to take to lift others around you?**

Chapter 6
FEEL GOOD

Exploring the Dimensions of Wellness

As I reflect on the evolution of my program since its inception in 2007, I have come to recognize the importance of expanding beyond the traditional Five Keys to Success. Through personal experience and growth, I have incorporated three additional areas that contribute to a well-rounded approach encompassing holistic wellness, the significance of our support systems, and the art of letting go. Central to it all is the imperative to feel good—a cornerstone in navigating life's myriad challenges, setbacks, and triumphs. For it's through mastering ourselves and our well-being that we pave the path to our greatest successes.

This book is a guide to practical strategies for achieving your dreams. Each aspiration you hold dear has its place in your lifelong journey, and feeling good isn't a one-size-fits-all concept. It's dynamic, influenced by the dimensions we focus on, the circumstances we face, and the phase of life we are in. This journey of well-being is ongoing, and our priorities may shift depending on the ebb and flow of life's currents.

In this chapter, I'll share personal anecdotes, insights, and actionable steps for cultivating wellness. The Global Wellness Institute defines wellness as "the active pursuit of activities, choices, and lifestyles that lead to a state of holistic health." While there are numerous dimensions of wellness identified in research and literature, I have chosen to concentrate on five key areas: physical, emotional, social, spiritual, and financial wellness. These dimensions serve as pillars supporting our overall well-being, each deserving of exploration and attention. So, let's delve deeper into each of them and uncover the pathways to feeling great in every aspect of our lives.

Physical wellness refers to the state of optimal health and well-being of the body, encompassing aspects such as fitness, nutrition, and overall bodily function.

CHAPTER 6: FEEL GOOD

From my early years, I discovered my affinity for movement through two activities that resonated deeply with me: swimming and racquetball. Despite not being naturally inclined towards athleticism, I found passion and a sense of achievement in these pursuits. Swimming, in particular, became a source of personal growth as I learned to set and surpass my own goals, one stroke at a time. Each practice session brought me closer to beating my personal records, teaching me the value of discipline and incremental improvement. The refreshing sensation of gliding through the water under the Southern Californian sun provided not only physical exertion but also mental clarity and relaxation.

Racquetball, with its fast-paced, competitive nature, further enhanced my physical wellness journey. It required quick reflexes, agility, and strategic thinking, challenging me both physically and mentally. Joining a local club and playing regularly with a younger neighbor not only improved my skills but also fostered a sense of camaraderie and community.

As life evolved, I recognized the importance of maintaining an active lifestyle, especially as I entered my fifties. Incorporating a regimen of regular walking, strength training, and hydration became paramount. Prioritizing preventive care, balanced nutrition, and adequate sleep has been foundational to my overall well-being. In Chapter 8, I will share a personal story of how diligence in preventive checkups proved to be lifesaving.

At elevink, we emphasize the importance of holistic wellness through our wellness session, which integrates corporate etiquette, superfoods, and mindfulness. Corporate etiquette training provides practical guidance on navigating professional settings with confidence and grace, ensuring individuals can present their best selves during corporate events and engagements. Here is how the training can help:

1. **Confidence Building:** Training can help you feel more confident in various social settings by teaching you the dos and don'ts.
2. **Communication Skills:** Learn effective communication techniques, including how to introduce yourself, engage in small talk, and exit conversations gracefully.
3. **Dining Etiquette:** Gain knowledge on proper dining etiquette, which is crucial for working lunches and formal dinners.
4. **Dress Code:** Understand appropriate dress codes for different events to ensure you always present yourself well.
5. **Cultural Awareness:** Learn about cultural differences and how to navigate international business settings respectfully.

Superfoods play a significant role in promoting physical wellness by offering nutrient-rich options that support overall health and vitality. From antioxidant-rich berries to omega-3-packed fatty fish, incorporating these powerhouse foods into our diets can help reduce the risk of chronic diseases, boost immunity, and support healthy aging.

As we embark on our journey towards physical wellness, it's essential to set personal goals and take actionable steps to enhance our well-being. **What are your aspirations for physical wellness, and what is one thing you can start doing today to move closer to achieving them?**

Whether it's committing to regular exercise, incorporating more superfoods into your diet, or prioritizing self-care practices, every small step counts towards a healthier, happier you.

Emotional wellness refers to the state of being in touch with, understanding, and effectively managing one's emotions in a healthy and balanced way.

Recognized for my high emotional intelligence, I have honed the ability to navigate stress, cultivate resilience, and nurture positive relationships. As you have read in previous chapters, my life has been a tapestry woven with diverse experiences. Amidst the ebb and flow of life's challenges, I have discovered a transformative practice that anchors me during moments of personal doubt: journaling.

Journaling serves as a powerful tool for self-reflection and emotional regulation. When I find myself coping with uncertainty or negative emotions, I turn to the pages of my journal. Here, I articulate the questions swirling in my mind, dissect the root causes of my feelings, and enumerate the blessings for which I am grateful. Mapping out actionable steps, listing possible research, and writing down a list of supportive individuals that I could outreach to, surrounds me with a sense of empowerment and perspective.

A pivotal exercise in defining my personal brand further reinforces my emotional wellness journey. By distilling my strengths, target audience, and unique value proposition into a concise statement, I have crafted a guiding beacon that anchors me in my purpose. My brand statement—"I am a trailblazer that drives vision to create opportunities for underrepresented talent"—embodies my commitment to opening doors for those who feel marginalized or unseen.

Moreover, investing in coaching and seeking guidance from experts has been instrumental in my personal and professional growth. When confronted with daunting challenges or new opportunities, enlisting the support of seasoned mentors and coaches has propelled me to new heights. For instance, the genesis of elevink—a culmination of my aspirations—was realized through an intensive workshop led by industry experts. Their guidance helped crystallize my business plan, define my niche, and visualize the trajectory of my dream company.

In Chapter 1, we talked about the importance of finding moments that bring us happiness. These moments are essential to our emotional wellness, helping us feel good from the inside out. Let's explore how to identify these blissful moments and the impact they can have on our lives.

Finding Your Bliss

To truly feel good, we need to recognize the activities or moments that make us feel joyful and content. Think about the times when you've done something and thought, "I could do this all day, every day, and be so happy." These activities are key to your emotional wellness because they come from within you. Relying on others to create these moments of happiness for you is less sustainable and less fulfilling.

The Power of Positivity

When you are happy, you attract more happiness. Have you noticed that when you're feeling good and smiling, good things tend to happen? You might find the perfect parking spot right in front of the store, or people may be more willing to help you. Your positive vibe spreads to others, and they respond in kind.

For example, I was once at the store in a rush and started to feel frustrated. I decided to change my mindset and asked a lady in line if I could go ahead of her because I had just a few minutes to get to my son's workplace to celebrate a milestone. Not only did she let me go ahead, but the people in front of her also let me pass. Instead of being stuck at the back of the line, I was quickly at the front, ready to buy balloons for my son's celebration. This small change in attitude led to a ripple effect of kindness and cooperation.

Avoiding Negative Triggers

While it's important to focus on what makes us happy, it's also crucial to recognize and avoid triggers that put us in a bad mood. Identify situations or behaviors that consistently make you feel negative and try to minimize them. Instead, seek out opportunities that make you happy and allow you to maintain a positive state of mind.

Practical Tools for Emotional Wellness

In the *From Dreams to Destiny* deck of cards, you'll find exercises and affirmations to help you maintain emotional balance and feel good. Here are a few practical activities to support your emotional wellness:

1. **Affirmations:** Use positive affirmations to start your day on the right foot. These can help shift your mindset and keep you focused on what brings you joy.
2. **Reflection:** Take time each day to reflect on what made you happy. Write down these moments and think about how you can incorporate more of them into your life.
3. **Gratitude:** Practice gratitude by acknowledging the good things in your life. This can be as simple as writing down three things you're thankful for each day.
4. **Mindfulness:** Engage in mindfulness practices like meditation or deep breathing exercises to stay grounded and centered.

By focusing on these activities, you'll find it easier to stay in a positive state of mind, which in turn attracts more positivity into your life.

Reflection prompts: **Do you have a brand statement that encapsulates your purpose and values?** When was the last time you revisited and refreshed it? Ensuring its relevance to your current endeavors can serve as a compass, guiding you towards alignment and fulfillment in your professional journey.

Social wellness refers to the quality of an individual's relationships and their ability to interact effectively with others within their community and society at large.

In Chapter 7, we will delve deeper into the vital importance of discovering our tribe and nurturing our social ecosystem. For now, I will provide a brief overview to pave the way for richer examples in the upcoming chapter. The relationships we cultivate throughout our various life stages play a pivotal role in maintaining our social wellness.

Having undergone personality tests, I have consistently found myself straddling the line between introversion and extroversion, leaning slightly towards the introverted end. Despite this, many who know me perceive me as an extrovert. This adaptability stems from my genuine enjoyment of human interaction and connection, although in smaller, more intimate settings. I cherish the opportunity to dedicate undivided attention to those I hold dear.

My relationships are neatly segmented into categories: school friends, work friends, and life friends. School friends are the comrades I met during my formative years, some dating back to middle and high school. Over four decades later, we still maintain semi-regular contact, coming together to celebrate milestones and share cherished memories. Work friends are those with whom I initially bonded over professional endeavors. Through shared experiences, such as weddings, births, promotions, and even illnesses, some of these connections have deepened into life friendships. Life friends are those who I met in my adult years and that cultivated intentionally in adulthood. These friends are my rock in every aspect of life, through the good times and the bad. They are the ones who stand by me when I need strength, offer a shoulder to lean on during difficult moments, and share in the joy of my successes. Their support is unwavering, providing a foundation of love and trust that I can always rely on.

Since moving to Florida in 2022, I find myself in the process of seeking out new friendships. It's a challenging endeavor to find individuals who align with my values and aspirations, yet I remain steadfast in my pursuit of quality relationships. Activities I enjoy partaking in with friends are varied and adaptable: from scenic hikes and leisurely strolls to cozy coffee dates and dinners. Whether it's completing workshops together, indulging in spa days, or simply sharing a heartfelt conversation over a glass of wine during a video call, the essence lies in our shared willingness to connect and spend meaningful time together.

In the next chapter, we'll explore these themes in greater depth, delving into specific anecdotes and examples that illuminate the profound impact of our social connections on our overall well-being.

How would you describe your social circle? Are you happy and fulfilled with your social wellness? What can you do to improve it?

Spiritual wellness refers to the sense of purpose, meaning, and connection to something greater than oneself.

Growing up in a non-religious household, my early exposure to spirituality was through Catholicism. Baptized and enrolled in a Catholic elementary school, I completed my first communion before our family's relocation to the northern part of Mexico when I was nine, and pretty much the relocation ended my religious activity. Despite this shift, my upbringing was immersed in the learning of metaphysics, thanks to my mother's collection of books on the subject. My beliefs gravitate towards the concept of the universe as a vast web of interconnected energy and as a result our actions, no matter how small, have a ripple effect on the universe, and every living entity. Through meditation and introspection, I discovered a profound sense of purpose—to be a servant leader—which has since guided my approach to life decisions with serenity and clarity. I am respectful of all beliefs, at the core of respecting all beliefs lies recognition of our shared humanity. Regardless of religious differences or beliefs, we all share common hopes, fears, joys, and sorrows. By embracing respect and understanding, I hope to foster a sense of unity and solidarity among diverse communities.

In 2020, I was granted the opportunity to participate in the transformative eight-week Mindfulness-Based Stress Reduction (MBSR) Program at the University of California San Diego Center for Mindfulness. This experience left an indelible mark on me, prompting me to incorporate mindfulness into the elevink wellness curriculum. Developed by Dr. Jon Kabat-Zinn, the MBSR Program is a meticulously structured course designed to equip participants with mindfulness skills to manage stress, alleviate anxiety, and enhance overall well-being. Throughout the program, we delved into a comprehensive array of practices and principles aimed at fostering mindfulness:

- **Weekly Sessions:** Led by trained instructors, these sessions provided a nurturing environment for participants to engage in various mindfulness exercises, from body scan meditations to mindful movement and sitting meditation.

- **Education and Discussion:** In addition to experiential practices, participants received valuable education on stress management, the mind-body connection, and the foundational principles of mindfulness.

- **Day of Mindfulness:** An extended session offered participants the opportunity to deepen their practice and integrate mindfulness into diverse aspects of their lives, fostering a profound sense of presence and resilience.

The ultimate aim of the MBSR Program is to empower participants to cultivate greater awareness, acceptance, and resilience in the face of life's myriad challenges. By honing mindfulness skills, individuals learn to navigate their experiences with clarity, compassion, and equanimity, thereby enhancing their overall well-being and quality of life. This journey towards inner peace and self-discovery continues to reverberate positively across all facets of my existence, shaping my interactions, decisions, and outlook on life.

How would you describe spiritual wellness? Have you ever practiced meditation or mindfulness? How do you find the quiet time you need to connect with your inner self?

Financial wellness refers to the state of one's overall financial health and stability. It encompasses the ability to effectively manage finances, make informed financial decisions, and maintain a sense of financial security and well-being.

As detailed in preceding chapters, my upbringing was rooted in a middle-class family, and my migration to the United States was marked by limited financial resources. Circumstances led me to embark on a career in the insurance industry at age fifteen. My journey began at the California-Mexico border, where I sold automobile insurance for vehicles traversing the border.

Subsequently, I transitioned to a prominent insurance company, specializing in auto and homeowners' policies. Upon settling in the United States, I obtained licensure from the state of California, enabling me to offer a comprehensive suite of personal coverage, including auto, home, life, and health insurance. This immersion in the insurance sector heightened my awareness of the criticality of financial protection.

Consider this: according to a 2020 survey by the American Psychological Association (APA), a staggering 64 percent of adults in the United States identified money as a significant source of stress in their lives. Similarly, the APA's 2021 Stress in America survey revealed that 56 percent of adults reported experiencing financial stress. Armed with this awareness, it becomes imperative to prioritize steps aimed at enhancing our financial wellness and alleviating stress in this domain.

Drawing from personal experience and expert insights (disclaimer: I am not a financial consultant and recommend consulting with experts), I have identified four pivotal decisions conducive to long-term financial planning and well-being:

1. **Budgeting:** Establishing a budget serves as the cornerstone of prudent financial management, providing clarity and discipline in spending habits.
2. **Real Estate Investment:** Investing in real estate offers a tangible asset that can appreciate over time, bolstering financial stability and wealth accumulation.
3. **Life Insurance:** Opting for life insurance policies with cash value accumulation provisions provides both protection and potential for long-term savings growth.
4. **Maximizing Employer Benefits:** Maximize contributions to a 401(k) retirement plan, leverage tuition reimbursement programs for educational expenses, and utilize discount programs in the purchase of goods and services.

CHAPTER 6: FEEL GOOD

Finally, maintaining an emergency savings fund and exploring low to medium-risk investment opportunities can further fortify financial resilience.

If you have not already, initiating a budget and conducting a comprehensive review of your financial objectives are paramount. Even seemingly insignificant expenses, such as a daily coffee habit, can accrue significantly over time—underscoring the importance of diligent financial management.

Conversations surrounding death or money within families may be deemed taboo in some cultural contexts. However, it's crucial to seek appropriate support and gather pertinent information to make informed decisions about our financial futures. Remember, it's never too early to start planning for long-term financial security and peace of mind.

When was the last time you sat down and created financial goals? Are you maximizing your employer contribution programs? How do you want to live when you retire? Are your loved ones protected?

In this chapter, I shared my personal journey of striving for holistic well-being by focusing on five key dimensions: physical, emotional, social, spiritual, and financial wellness. I recounted how dedicating attention to each of these aspects of wellness has positively impacted my life and helped me achieve my goals.

In exploring physical wellness, I discussed my commitment to regular exercise, nutritious eating habits, and adequate rest, emphasizing how prioritizing my physical health has boosted my energy levels, resilience, and overall vitality.

I delved into emotional wellness by reflecting on my

journey towards self-awareness, emotional regulation, and cultivating healthy coping mechanisms. I shared how practices like journaling, and seeking support have empowered me to navigate life's challenges with greater ease and resilience.

In discussing social wellness, I recounted the importance of nurturing meaningful connections with family, friends, and communities. I highlighted how fostering positive relationships, practicing empathy, and engaging in social activities have enriched my life and provided a strong support system.

Spiritual wellness emerged as a cornerstone of my well-being journey, as I explored my sense of purpose, meaning, and connection to something greater than myself. I shared how practices like meditation, reflection, and embracing gratitude have deepened my spiritual awareness and contributed to a sense of inner peace and fulfillment.

Lastly, I emphasized the significance of financial wellness in achieving life goals and maintaining overall well-being. I discussed my efforts to budget effectively, save for the future, and cultivate a healthy relationship with money, underscoring how financial stability has provided a sense of security and freedom to pursue my passions and aspirations.

Overall, I illustrated how caring for each dimension of wellness holistically has been instrumental in realizing my life goals, fostering personal growth, and cultivating a balanced and fulfilling life. By prioritizing physical, emotional, social, spiritual, and financial well-being, I have found greater harmony, resilience, and fulfillment on my wellness journey, and I hope you too can do the same.

In the *From Dreams to Destiny Diary*, we have a space dedicated to rate each of the dimensions and outline actionable steps and phased goals that can help you achieve the next level.

Chapter 7
FIND YOUR TRIBE

Discovering Your Supportive Network

Personal Story No. 1: Mexico City (1995-1996), PIE Model

The nine months I lived in Mexico City were nine months of pure happiness. It was a short but rich experience that allowed me to soak in the city's vibrant atmosphere, enjoying plays and art festivals. After my husband completed his social service in medicine in Zipolite, we moved to Mexico City for two specialized courses he was enrolled in at a medical school. Thanks to his family's furnished apartment in the well-situated Colonia del Valle, our transition was smooth.

We arrived on a Sunday, and I immediately went out to buy a newspaper to start job hunting. In 1995, that was how you found jobs. According to bts.gov, Mexico City, then a city of 16 million people (now 22.5 million), had excellent infrastructure and public transportation. Buses, light buses, subways, taxis, and light trains made it easy to get around.

Having never lived in or visited Mexico City before, I searched for job ads for roles like bilingual secretary or assistant, focusing on locations close to our apartment or easily accessible. To my surprise, I had several interviews that week with three international companies and received two job offers. I chose Bank of America in the financial district. My role was to support the vice president of finance, an expatriate from Newark, New Jersey. Little did I know that eighteen years later, I would find myself in Newark for another job opportunity.

Excited to join such a prestigious firm, I quickly made new friends, many of whom I still keep in touch with. Initially, my tasks were simple, so I finished them quickly and started asking how I could help or learn more. The response was overwhelmingly positive, with everyone being very helpful. I suggested a few process changes to streamline tasks, which were well-received.

CHAPTER 7: FIND YOUR TRIBE

One day, someone overheard me speaking English with my boss and asked if I could call the United States Bank of America office to relay a message. Delighted to help, I soon found myself making calls for various people and departments, learning about the business through these translations and follow-ups.

At the same time, I enrolled at Centro Mexicano Americano de Relaciones Culturales (CEMARC) for an English as a Second Language teacher certification. In my six-hour weekly class, I made a close friend. We spent breaks and lunch together, and she visited us in California in 2002 when my son was born. We kept in touch for many years but eventually lost contact. I still think of her fondly, as she was instrumental in my early introspection and meditation practices.

In Mexico City, I found my tribe—a group of people who included me in lunches, celebrated birthdays with me, gave me rides home in the rain, and helped me navigate when roads were closed due to political protests. When it was time to leave, I received flowers, books, and heartfelt farewells from my new friends and coworkers.

This experience highlights the importance of image and exposure, as described in Harvey Coleman's Performance, Image and Exposure (PIE) model, which I later learned about while completing my master's degree. Unknowingly, I had used the PIE model to succeed in my role in Mexico City by fostering a collaborative image and gaining exposure through my international calls. This model became a fundamental practice in my corporate roles, especially when I moved to New Jersey and joined a global finance industry.

Uprooting our family of five, selling our home, and taking on a new job in a different state across the country was not easy. In 2013, we embarked on a new journey, moving from California to New Jersey. The coast-to-coast journey was filled with mixed feelings and new challenges, which I will share in Chapter 8.

Personal Story No. 2: New Jersey (2013-2022), Networking, Strategic Vision, and Alliances

When I arrived in New Jersey, I made a commitment to myself: to truly show up and to embrace all outcomes of taking action. I aimed to avoid self-sabotage and to create a lasting legacy that would support Hispanic growth in corporate America. I was eager to find my Hispanic, Latino tribe on the East Coast.

On my second day at my new job, I researched the business resource group that supported Hispanics and signed up. Within six months of joining an organization with thousands of employees across various countries over Asia, Europe and Latin America, I was nominated and selected as co-lead of the Hispanic Business Resource Group. My role was to develop a strategy that would support the growth and development of Hispanic employees in the group and impact the community and market strategies. At the time, the group had about 300 members.

My co-lead was a young, intelligent, and enthusiastic Hispanic based in Minneapolis. Together, we created strategies to recruit more Hispanics to our business resource group. In just two years, the group grew from three hundred to over one thousand employees. I then stepped down to create growth opportunities for others, and as I shared in my keynote speech of **"How to Go From Invisible to Unstoppable,"** I created a new strategic role as Hispanic Initiatives Officer, focusing on building strong external relationships.

This chapter is about finding your tribe and assessing your network as part of your overall success. As I expanded my connections outside the organization and formed strategic alliances, the impact was significant. Here, I will focus on four major alliances, some briefly previously mentioned in Chapter 5:

Hispanics Inspiring Students' Performance and Achievement (HISPA): This nonprofit organization aims to bring role models to schools so Hispanic kids can see themselves represented through professional role models. HISPA has a Role Model Program, ensuring a consistent approach to presenting stories in classrooms. I became a role model, visiting middle schools in New Jersey to share my story in English and Spanish. The deep, intelligent questions from students were enlightening. I realized that this could be a win-win situation: exposing business resource group members to community service would help retain and grow our talent pipeline while impacting future generations. The first year was a success, enrolling and training dozens of role models. I then secured an executive sponsor to host a HISPA corporate visit, allowing students to visit our office, interact with professionals, and learn about the company. This opportunity brought fulfilling moments for all of us, and I continue to support HISPA through their South Florida council. My relationship with the CEO and founder opened up other opportunities of further collaboration, such as sharing my personal journey with students in Princeton University.

The Red Shoe Movement: The Red Shoe Movement, a leadership development company powered by a global community of professionals who support each other for career success with the mission of increasing female representation in leadership. At their annual conference, I was inspired by the meaningful Mutual Mentoring Circles and envisioned bringing this methodology to our company. At the end of the session, participants paired up to write down their goals. I wrote two: becoming a vice president and chief of staff, and bringing the mutual mentoring circles to our organization. Within a couple of years, I achieved both.

Implementing the Red Shoe Movement methodology was challenging as it was a new concept to be socialized, and vetted, but we contracted the company's services for a Train-the-Trainer program to be able to roll out the Mutual Mentoring Circles in my organization. I then worked closely with the executive sponsor of our business resource group, a strong Latina professional who I admire. I put together a proposal, supported by data, and with her backing I kicked off the Circles. I created a committee of leaders, completed train-the-trainers workshops, developed surveys, and set up quarterly reporting metrics. We shared our progress on social media, generating excitement. Soon, higher executives were eager to facilitate the circles, and we gained recognition outside the United States.

I shared the model during a visit to Brazil and was invited as a keynote speaker by the Mexico Investment Office in 2020, a few blocks from where I started as a bilingual assistant at Bank of America. During International Women's day, I still participate in the Red Shoe Movement yearly "Ring the Bell on the 7 Seas." The global celebration includes bell-ringing ceremonies that call for more women in decision-making positions, equal pay for equal work, and equal distribution of power.

We Are All Human Foundation and Hispanic Star: As one of the twenty-five founding members of the Hispanic Star Alliance, I have participated in several Hispanic Leadership Summits hosted in the United Nations and supported the Hispanic Promise 2.0 Execution Framework, a guide for corporate organizations to develop, hire, retain, promote, celebrate Hispanics, and buy from Hispanic providers. Major milestones included recognizing 65 Hispanic Stars on a Times Square billboard and providing free financial wellness access to thousands of Hispanics through partnerships with professional Hispanic organizations. This was not a solo achievement but the result of a strong network and common goals. I am still very vested and continue to support the

Hispanic Star mission. As a way to generate a larger impact at the local level, I volunteered to lead the Hispanic Star Tampa Hub, and look forward to having a profound impact in our community.

Today's Inspired Latina and Young Latina Talks: My participation in *Today's Inspired Latina Vol. 5* introduced me to an inspirational tribe. Along with twenty-five other authors, we formed unbreakable bonds, sharing our journeys at events like the New York Times and Estee Lauder. Motivated by this experience, I took on the national director role of Young Latina Talks. I brought the Young Latina Talks to the tristate area of New York, New Jersey, and Connecticut in September of 2020 in the midst of a pandemic. Shortly after we also rolled out the program in Cicero, Illinois. I was able to engage sponsors, and the programs were a success due to the support and dedication of Jackie Camacho Ruiz, who is the creator and main sponsor of the program, as well as the amazing and dedicated public speaking trainer. The outcome is impactful, twelve Young Latinas finding their tribe, finding the support system to share their journey in a stage and enhancing their public speaking skills.

These experiences highlight the power of showing up, building a supportive network, and creating lasting impacts within and beyond the organization.

Personal Story No. 3: The Impact of Mentors and Sponsors

In the previous stories, I emphasized the importance of executive sponsors in achieving success and making an impact. Executive sponsors help remove obstacles and provide necessary resources to achieve goals. In my experience, to effectively leverage their support, it's essential to present a clear proposal with well-defined outcomes. The request must be precise so they know exactly how to assist. This aligns with the lesson from Chapter 1: having clarity in our North Star is crucial.

I would like to share three more examples—one involving a mentor, the other a sponsor, and the final example being a once in a lifetime supporter—illustrating how their support was critical to my career aspirations.

As I settled into my role in New Jersey and co-leadership of the Hispanic Resource Group, I set a new goal in 2015 to work in the international area with a focus on Latin America. When I shared this goal with my mentor, she helped me connect dots I hadn't considered. The executive sponsor of the Hispanic Resource Group was a global leader with international responsibilities. She suggested he might help me understand the roles in that space. Shortly after, a relevant role became available. I applied, and he put in a good word for me based on my work in diversity, equity, and inclusion (DEI). This demonstrates the PIE model in action—exposure through DEI work led to this opportunity.

About two years into my new international role, I was selected for a pilot program where high-level executives were paired with junior executives for coaching. During the interview with the Talent Development Office, I kept my answers professional and aligned with my role. However, at the end, as I have shared in my keynote of **"The Art of Risk Taking,"** I felt compelled to share my true aspiration: to work hands-on in the international operations of the company. This is another example of the importance of being clear about our goals, and our willingness to take on risks. She thanked me for my honesty and later informed me I had been paired with the regional vice president of Europe and Latin America international operations.

As our mentoring and coaching sessions unfolded over the following months, I experienced the true power of sponsorship. My mentor took the initiative to call my manager and request 30 to 40 percent of my time for a special project in Brazil. Finally, an opportunity that had been in my personal vision board for years manifested! This highlights the power of clarity in our goals, networking, mentoring, and sponsorship.

However, it's important to note that networking should not be transactional or one-sided. Networking is about building genuine relationships based on trust, shared values, mutual understanding, and a desire for mutual success.

I hope you can start to see how clarity in personal goals and a strong network are interlinked, presenting new opportunities and helping to achieve them. Let me emphasize the past simple examples to illustrate this point.

When I expressed my goal of working internationally, my mentor connected me with opportunities. This led to an invitation to participate in a project in Brazil. While working with the Brazil team, I shared the Red Shoe Movement circles, which fostered further expansion of the methodology to their office and further new connections. One of these connections was the Global Human Resources leader who participated in a mentoring circle. She then introduced the idea of me coming to Mexico as a keynote speaker. A full end-to-end circle example.

The most remarkable example in this segment is this one. I consider myself incredibly fortunate, as not everyone gets the chance to cultivate a professional relationship that not only lasts but grows stronger over the course of twenty-four years. Throughout these twenty-four years, I have been privileged to receive the guidance, support, and leadership of someone who is generous, exceptionally intelligent, driven by excellence, humorous, and encouraging. This remarkable leader has undoubtedly transformed the trajectory of my career, believing in me through all my strengths and weaknesses, and demonstrating the wisdom and flexibility to allow me to be my authentic self. Stretching me, and putting me out of my comfort zone on many occasions.

When this relationship began, her management style was prescriptive and directive. Over time, it evolved into a guiding and progressive approach, then into one that was supportive and encouraging, and eventually into a style that was trustful and collaborative. Thanks to her leadership, I have experienced significant professional and personal growth, sharing some of my most thrilling achievements as well as my most vulnerable moments.

This leader's impact has been profound, not just on my career but on my entire life. Her influence has extended beyond professional boundaries, affecting my family in the most positive ways. We will forever be grateful for the difference she has made in our lives.

The chain of most of my life events highlights the power of a supportive network and the importance of clear goals. Each relationship and opportunity built upon the last, creating a momentum that propelled me forward in my career.

I break down my tribe and support system into four key groups:

1. Relatives and Close Friends

These are the people we can count on for personal support. They act as our personal board of directors, challenging us, providing feedback, and helping us become the best versions of ourselves. These individuals love us genuinely and share their honest thoughts with us.

2. Local Support and Network

This includes people from our local circles, such as those we meet through our kids' activities, sports associations, and volunteer work. These connections are essential for building a sense of community and local support.

3. Professional Network

These are the colleagues we interact with daily, creating positive relationships through collaboration. By being good listeners and understanding their goals, we can offer valuable support and build a strong professional network.

4. Strategic Network Alliances

This group consists of individuals who help propel us toward our larger dreams. They include executive supporters who trust our vision and are willing to back our ideas with their name and resources. Their belief in our abilities and the impact we create together is invaluable.

Networking can be daunting for some, but understanding its importance is crucial. In the previous chapter, I discussed the significance of creating your personal brand. Now, I would like to stress the importance of having your elevator pitch. These are two useful tools to help you navigate the networking arena and clarify the types of relationships and alliances you seek.

Take a moment to assess your current support network. **Who has supported you without you realizing they acted as a mentor or sponsor? Why is a support network and finding your tribe essential for achieving your personal goals?** In the *From Dreams to Destiny Diary* there is a section dedicated to assess your network, identify gaps in it, and document who else you need on board.

In *Today's Inspired Latina*, I used the quote: "Surround yourself with those that believe in the beauty of your dreams." This means having a tribe and support system because we are not meant to do things alone.

The importance of networking cannot be overstated. It's not just about making connections but fostering genuine relationships based on trust and mutual goals. Having a clear vision and an elevator pitch can help navigate this process effectively. Reflect on your current network. Identify those who have supported you and think about how you can strengthen these relationships. Remember, achieving your goals often requires the help of a supportive network.

Here are three practical activities to help you put the concepts from this chapter into practice:

PIE Model

In his 1996 book, *Empower Yourself: The Organizational Game Revealed*, Harvey J. Coleman coined the concept Performance, Image, and Exposure (PIE) Model to uncover the fallacy that ascending the hierarchy of an organization was heavily dictated by performance and little weight given to other factors. Let's dive deeper into the PIE Model. According to Coleman, your career success is not just about how well you perform your tasks but also about how others perceive you and how much exposure you get. Here's a breakdown:

1. **Performance (10 percent):** This involves the day-to-day work you're assigned and the quality of the results you deliver. While important, it only accounts for a small part of your career success.
2. **Image (30 percent):** This is about what others think of you—your personal brand. Do you maintain a positive attitude? Are you seen as someone who provides solutions or as someone who only points out problems?
3. **Exposure (60 percent):** This is the most significant part of the model. It's about who knows you and what you do. Does your boss know your contributions? Do their superiors? Do people both inside and outside your organization know your work?

Elevator Pitch

An elevator pitch is a brief (about 30 seconds) way of introducing yourself, highlighting key points, and making a connection with someone. It's called an elevator pitch because it should take roughly the same amount of time as an elevator ride. Having a good elevator pitch is crucial. When you meet someone or have an opportunity to connect and ask for collaboration, you need to express succinctly what you need. The clearer and more concise you are, the easier it is for the other person to understand and either help you or refer you to the right person.

Example Exercise:

1. **Draft Your Pitch:** Write a 30-second summary about who you are, what you do, and what you need.
2. **Practice:** Rehearse it until you can deliver it smoothly and confidently.
3. **Test It:** Try it out in real situations and tweak it based on feedback and your experience.

Network Assessment

In the *From Dreams to Destiny Diary*, there's an exercise for assessing your current network and identifying what you need. Here's a deeper look:

Your network should include people from all stages of your career. It should be diverse, with individuals who have different backgrounds, experiences, and skills. This diversity enhances your perspective and helps you stretch your imagination.

Example Exercise:

1. **List Your Contacts:** Write down people in your network from various phases of your career.

2. **Identify Gaps:** Look for areas where you lack connections—perhaps in different industries or roles.
3. **Reach Out:** Make an effort to connect with new people who can provide different insights and opportunities.

Taking risks is a crucial part of achieving personal goals for several key reasons:

1. **Growth and Learning**

- **Experience:** Taking risks often leads to new experiences that expand your knowledge and skills. Even if you fail, you learn valuable lessons that can help you in future endeavors.
- **Adaptability:** Facing risks and overcoming challenges makes you more adaptable and resilient, preparing you for unforeseen obstacles.

2. **Opportunities**

- **Unseen Opportunities:** Many opportunities are hidden behind a veil of risk. By taking risks, you can uncover possibilities that you wouldn't have encountered otherwise.
- **Innovation:** Risk-taking encourages creative thinking and innovation. It pushes you to think outside the box and find unique solutions.

3. **Achieving Greater Success**

- **Higher Rewards:** Greater risks often come with the potential for greater rewards. If you only take safe bets, you may miss out on significant achievements and breakthroughs.
- **Pushing Limits:** Taking risks helps you push beyond your comfort zone, enabling you to achieve goals that might seem unattainable initially.

4. **Building Confidence**
- **Self-Efficacy:** Successfully navigating risks builds confidence in your abilities. Each time you take a risk and succeed, you reinforce your belief in your capacity to handle challenges.
- **Empowerment:** Taking control of your destiny by making bold choices empowers you and strengthens your resolve to pursue your goals.

5. **Avoiding Regret**
- **No Regrets:** Taking risks minimizes the chances of looking back with regret, wondering "what if?" It's better to try and to fail than to never try at all and be left with uncertainty about what could have been.
- **Life Satisfaction:** People who take risks often report higher levels of life satisfaction. The pursuit of meaningful goals, even with associated risks, can lead to a more fulfilling life.

Practical Examples
- **Career Change:** Switching careers involves risk, but it can lead to a more fulfilling and prosperous professional life.
- **Starting a Business:** Launching a new business is risky, but it can bring immense personal satisfaction and financial success if it succeeds.
- **Personal Development:** Trying new hobbies or learning new skills can be risky in terms of time and effort, but it enriches your life and can lead to personal growth.

Are you taking enough risks to achieve your dreams? How are you evaluating risks as they present themselves?

To achieve success and make the most of opportunities, it's crucial to have a clear understanding of your personal goals and a robust support network. The PIE Model demonstrates that excelling in your field is not enough on its own; how others perceive you and your visibility are equally important. Crafting a strong elevator pitch helps you to communicate your goals and needs effectively, while a thorough network assessment ensures you have the right connections to support your ambitions. Taking risks is essential for personal growth, discovering new opportunities, achieving significant success, building confidence, and avoiding regret. Risks can be daunting, but they are often necessary to move beyond the status quo and reach your full potential. By understanding and embracing the importance of risk-taking, you can more effectively pursue and achieve your personal goals.

Remember, surrounding yourself with people who believe in the beauty of your dreams is key. As highlighted in Today's Inspired Latina, we are not meant to achieve great things alone. Your tribe and support system are essential for turning your dreams into reality. By taking calculated risks and building a strong support network, you position yourself to turn your dreams into destiny.

Chapter 8
LET GO

Release and Renewal

As we reach the final chapter of this book, I feel an overwhelming sense of gratitude for the journey I have undertaken. Life has been challenging, but it also has given me the chance to consciously turn things around, adapt to changing circumstances, and take risks that have shaped both my future and my family's. I often wish I could be thirty again, but with the knowledge I have today. The core purpose of this book is to share with younger generations, or anyone looking to reinvent themselves, that it's never too late to start or to change course. We owe it to ourselves to pursue our dreams.

This chapter is about allowing experiences to unfold and trusting that everything will work out for the best. Let me share some personal stories, beginning with two homes that despite all odds were meant to be ours.

As I mentioned in earlier chapters, in 2013, we decided to move to New Jersey for an opportunity with a global financial company. During the interview process and final contract stages, my husband and I visited New Jersey to explore cities near the office. We wanted the best public education for our children, a low-crime rate, and proximity to work. We eventually chose Montville, a beautiful small town in the suburbs of Newark, New Jersey. After visiting several homes for sale, we found one that seemed perfect for our family. We made an offer and negotiated the final details during our cross-country trip from California to New Jersey.

For some reason, we decided not to show pictures of the home to our kids, planning to surprise them once we got the keys. But that day never came. When we went for the final inspection before signing the final purchase papers, we discovered new damage to the home and missing items like the washer and dryer. The appliances had been replaced with cheaper versions. We couldn't accept the property, leaving us stranded in a new city without a permanent address.

CHAPTER 8: LET GO

Without a permanent address, we faced numerous challenges. We couldn't get new driver's licenses, open a post office box, or enroll the kids in school. Our situation was temporary, but it made me realize how difficult it is for those without a stable address. One caring lady from the school district found a solution for us, and thanks to her support, we managed to start settling in.

We stayed in a small, pet-friendly hotel for the next two months. Feeling disappointed, lonely, and lost, we restarted our home search. This time, I had just started a new job, so I could not visit potential homes. I had to let go and trust my husband and our realtor to find the right place for our family. My husband has great taste so I was confident he would select only what was best for all of us. They narrowed it down to the top two options and eventually chose one. When I finally walked into the home, I knew it was meant for us. It was newer, bigger, and better than the original one. This experience reaffirmed my belief that everything happens for a reason, and if we trust that it's for the best, the universe will manifest a better outcome.

During our hotel stay, I learned to let go and enjoy the moment. I appreciated not having to cook or clean and made the most of the free breakfasts. We bought new clothes, shoes, and backpacks since all our belongings were in storage in Baltimore. Some might have seen our situation as chaotic and regrettable, but I look back on it as a lesson in trust and faith that everything works out.

In no time, we settled into our new home. The kids each had their own room, and we made a few upgrades to create a beautiful childhood home where they made great memories. When we built the basement, I even had a special area built to host workshops and support the community, which brought me a lot of happiness. This home provided us with safety and space during the 2020 pandemic, solidifying our belief that it was meant to be.

Nine years later, we found ourselves in a similarly dramatic situation. Since 2018, we had been considering a move to Florida for two main reasons: to evaluate it as a potential retirement location and to reduce our expenses to fully fund our three sons' bachelor's degrees. We visited various areas in South Florida and Northeast Florida, and during our spring break in 2022, we decided that the Tampa Bay area was the best fit. Tampa Bay's gross domestic product (GDP) increased by 4.9 percent in 2022; it hasn't been hit by a major hurricane since 1921; and it has a local state university with significant investments and growth opportunities.

Next, we needed to decide whether to live north or south of Tampa, so we asked our real estate professional to help us explore both areas. The real estate market in 2022 was booming, with low interest rates that were expected to rise, and homes were selling rapidly. According to the U.S. Census Bureau, 319,000 new residents moved to Florida in 2022—the largest influx in the country—making it the fastest-growing state since 1957. Given this, we had to act quickly and make higher-than-listed offers on homes. We wanted a house north of Tampa with specific features: proximity to A-rated schools, office space, and family amenities. The inventory was low and competition fierce. My husband was constantly on the lookout for properties. We finally found a suitable home in one of the local areas we visited. Imagine this: we made an offer over the phone and negotiated all the details from New Jersey, without ever seeing the home in person.

Meanwhile, we put our house in New Jersey up for sale and began negotiating both deals. On the day of the new Florida home inspection, my husband had a plane ticket to attend, but his flight was canceled, and the next one wasn't available until the evening, making it impossible for him to be there. Thanks to technology, we asked the inspector to conduct a virtual walk-through. We had to trust that this was the right home for us.

CHAPTER 8: LET GO

The transition was challenging. We left New Jersey mid-July after the kids finished school and for a few weeks temporarily lived in Orlando at a timeshare we owned. When we took possession of the new property—a home we bought virtually without setting foot in—it turned out to be everything we had hoped for, but our movers had damaged most of our possessions. Despite this setback, we managed to enroll the kids in soccer and swimming, and they started their new school year a few weeks after our arrival. Francisco, our oldest son, transferred from New Jersey to the University of South Florida and moved into a university apartment shortly after.

Dealing with replacing the damaged personal property, the moving company, insurance, and helping two teenagers adjust to a new area was tough. However, I realized that the damaged items were replaceable, and I had to let go and embrace this new chapter. I began taking morning walks in the beautiful Florida nature, journaling, meditating, and practicing gratitude for our new home, my new job and this new environment that is meant to be the platform of the next stage in our life.

Now, our kids have graduated—one from college and one from high school, and our youngest was accepted into a rigorous International Baccalaureate program. After nearly two years of living here, I can confidently say we made the right decision. By accepting things as they are, rather than wishing they were different, I have learned to enjoy the present. My current reality is seeing my kids healthy and successful, and having the opportunity to write a book, which was once only a distant dream!

A Journey of Survival and Hope

Early in 2021, during my annual checkup, I had a mammogram that yielded unusual results. Immediately, I was assigned a breast cancer navigator who compassionately explained the next steps. Even though I did not work directly in the medical field, my experience in the disability insurance industry made the diagnosis and treatment somewhat familiar. I firmly believe in preventive medicine, so taking the recommended tests at the suggested age was non-negotiable for me. I took the news with calmness and positivity, reflecting on my life and feeling content with what I had accomplished and the lives I had touched. If this was the end, I felt I was leaving in a good place, though I did feel a deep nostalgia for those I might leave behind.

As a Type A personality, I like to control outcomes and move things along quickly and efficiently. But in this new situation, I had to find a breast surgeon, an oncologist, and navigate an entirely new cancer center ecosystem. Having my husband's support, his medical knowledge, and his ability to find the right providers was priceless. I had to trust the process, learn to let go, and be patient and flexible.

In May 2021, I underwent the first surgery to remove the malignant cells. As I write this book, it has been three years since the surgery, and I am happy to share that I am cancer-free. I celebrate my life for this milestone. As I shared in my keynote speech of **"Say Yes to Yourself,"** while recovering from the first surgery, the role of VP and Chief of staff that I had been aspiring for became available and without hesitation I applied and interviewed for it. I was offered the job, which started in June. This role required 100% of my mental agility, decision-making, execution, and leadership skills. However, after the second surgery in October 2021, and the beginning of a more extensive treatment, I realized the demands of my new job, physical surgery, emotional illness recovery, and daily life activities were too much to handle.

For the first time in my life, I felt anxious, hopeless, physically, and mentally drained, and unable to multitask across different aspects of my life. As a high performer and high achiever, I saw this as a weakness. In a moment of vulnerability, I shared my feelings with my husband, who has always been by my side to support me. We agreed that for the next few months, I would focus solely on my personal needs and my new role. My personal needs also meant having the support of an online therapist who helped me cope.

For about two months, I put aside kid's activities, household chores and any decision-making outside of work to prioritize my health. I had not realized the burden I placed on myself. I had not taken the necessary time to grieve my diagnosis, to fully heal before jumping into new, demanding professional responsibilities without giving me any grace. My mental health suffered until I let go of my ego to recognize I was not doing well and asked for help. In just a few months, after a holiday visit to California where I was pampered by friends and family, I went back to closing this chapter and feeling like myself again, and maybe feeling stronger than ever.

This is how early 2022, after a full recovery we made a major decision: it was time to move to Florida and start the new chapter we had envisioned. The universe provides us with the tools, resources, experiences, and knowledge at the right time, but we have to trust and let go to accept what is destined for us.

The title of this book is *From Dreams to Destiny*, and as I reflect on my personal stories and journey, I see that the past thirty years of experiences were meant to bring me to this moment. The eight chapters of this book take on a life of their own, epitomizing the fundamental lessons I have learned. I fully believe in the power of these teachings. While they are my personal experiences, I guarantee that each one can bring you closer to your destination, the destination you have dreamed of. Whether you are in your twenties or your sixties, you can apply these practical guides immediately.

I do not know if I would have recognized the importance of letting go if I had not faced the pain and fear of a cancer diagnosis or the ambiguity of being temporarily homeless in new cities where we had no support system at all, with three kids, and a pet. These experiences helped me to appreciate the beauty and blessing of homeownership and the importance of a strong ecosystem of professional and personal relationships.

We moved to Florida, where I found a top-tier cancer center to monitor my progress. Through them, I completed genetic testing, which came back negative, giving me confidence that I am not predestined to get cancer and have some control over my health. I accepted a new professional role that allowed me to take on new opportunities and expand my skills. I also embraced a leadership role in diversity, equity, and inclusion, the State of Women commission in my county, and the newly created Tampa Hispanic Star Hub. I became an active member of the South Florida HISPA council and received the support to bring this book, diary, and deck of cards to life.

Every experience, opportunity, challenge, success, and relationship has come together to create a new version of me. I continue to reinvent myself using the eight steps to success, and I am excited about the future.

Practical Applications of What We Cover in This Chapter

Maintaining good health, both physically and mentally, is essential for a fulfilling life. Women, in particular, face unique health challenges that necessitate proactive health checkups. Alongside this, the ability to practice letting go, prioritize mental health, and understand different personality types can significantly enhance overall well-being. This guide will detail the importance of these aspects and offer practical steps to achieve them.

Proactive Health Checkups for Women

Proactive health checkups are critical for early detection and prevention of diseases, particularly those that disproportionately affect women, such as breast and cervical cancer. Regular screenings can identify health issues before they become severe, allowing for more effective treatment and better outcomes. Additionally, these checkups provide an opportunity to discuss lifestyle choices, reproductive health, and any concerns with a healthcare provider, fostering a holistic approach to health.

Practical Steps

1. **Schedule Regular Appointments**
   - Annual checkups with a primary care physician.
   - Regular visits to a gynecologist for reproductive health screenings, including Pap smears and HPV tests.
   - Schedule mammograms as recommended by your physician (generally starting at age 40 or earlier if there is a family history of breast cancer).

2. **Stay Informed**
   - Understand the recommended health screenings for your age group and medical history.
   - Keep track of vaccination schedules and flu shots.

3. **Maintain Health Records**
   - Keep a personal health record of past checkups, test results, and any treatments.
   - Share this information with all healthcare providers to ensure coordinated care.

4. **Adopt a Healthy Lifestyle**
   - Engage in regular physical activity.
   - Eat a balanced diet rich in fruits, vegetables, and whole grains.
   - Avoid smoking and limit alcohol consumption.

5. **Practice Preventive Measures**
   - Perform regular self-exams, such as breast self-exams.
   - Monitor any changes in your body and report them to your doctor immediately.

Letting Go Practices

Letting go of stress, unrealistic expectations, and past traumas is crucial for mental health and emotional well-being. Holding onto negative emotions and trying to control every aspect of life can lead to chronic stress, anxiety, and burnout. Practicing letting go can foster resilience, peace of mind, and a better quality of life.

Practical Steps

1. **Mindfulness and Meditation**
   - Practice mindfulness to stay present and reduce overthinking.
   - Meditate regularly to calm the mind and release tension.

2. **Acceptance**
   - Accept situations and outcomes that are beyond your control.
   - Focus on what you can change and let go of what you cannot.

3. Set Boundaries
    - Learn to say no to commitments that add unnecessary stress.
    - Protect your time and energy by setting clear personal boundaries.

4. Journaling
    - Write about your feelings and experiences to process emotions.
    - Use journaling as a tool to identify and release negative thoughts.

5. Physical Activity
    - Engage in physical activities like yoga or tai chi that promote relaxation and stress relief.
    - Exercise regularly to boost endorphins and improve mood.

6. Seek Support
    - Talk to a trusted friend, family member, or therapist about your struggles.
    - Join support groups to connect with others who understand your experiences.

Maintaining Mental Health a Priority

Mental health is as important as physical health. Poor mental health can affect every aspect of life, including relationships, work, and physical well-being. Prioritizing mental health ensures a balanced life, improves productivity, and fosters better relationships.

Practical Steps

1. **Regular Mental Health Check-ins**
   - Schedule regular appointments with a mental health professional.
   - Use mental health apps to monitor mood and stress levels.

2. **Healthy Habits**
   - Ensure adequate sleep, aiming for seven to nine hours per night.
   - Maintain a balanced diet and stay hydrated.
   - Exercise regularly to reduce stress and improve mood.

3. **Stress Management**
   - Practice deep breathing exercises and progressive muscle relaxation.
   - Allocate time for hobbies and activities that bring joy.

4. **Social Connections**
   - Maintain strong relationships with friends and family.
   - Participate in community activities and volunteer work.

5. **Limit Screen Time**
   - Reduce time spent on social media and news, which can increase stress and anxiety.
   - Unplug from digital devices regularly to recharge.

6. Professional Help
   - Seek therapy or counseling if dealing with persistent stress, anxiety, or depression.
   - Consider medication if prescribed by a healthcare provider for managing mental health conditions.

Understanding Type A and B Personalities
Type A Personality

Characteristics:
- Highly competitive and goal-oriented
- Time-conscious and punctual
- Inclined towards multitasking and high productivity
- Prone to stress and impatience

Challenges:
- Risk of burnout due to high stress levels
- Difficulty in relaxing and enjoying leisure time
- Potential strain on relationships due to perfectionism and impatience

Practical Steps:
1. Balance Work and Leisure
   - Schedule regular breaks and leisure activities.
   - Prioritize downtime to recharge.

2. Stress Management
   - Practice relaxation techniques like deep breathing and meditation.
   - Delegate tasks to reduce workload and stress.

3. **Realistic Goal Setting**
   - Set achievable goals and celebrate small wins.
   - Avoid overcommitting and set realistic expectations.

4. **Develop Patience**
   - Practice patience by engaging in activities that require slow progress, like gardening or puzzles.
   - Reflect on the importance of enjoying the journey, not just the destination.

Type B Personality

Characteristics:
- Relaxed and easy-going
- Less focused on competition and more on enjoying life
- Patient and even-tempered
- Generally less stressed and more flexible

Challenges:
- Potential lack of urgency in achieving goals
- May be perceived as lacking ambition or drive
- Risk of procrastination and poor time management

Practical Steps:

1. **Structured Planning**
   - Use planners or digital tools to organize tasks and set deadlines.
   - Break larger goals into smaller, manageable steps.

2. Motivation
    - Find sources of inspiration and motivation to stay focused on goals.
    - Set personal challenges to push beyond comfort zones.

3. Time Management
    - Prioritize tasks based on importance and deadlines.
    - Practice discipline in adhering to schedules and timelines.

4. Balancing Relaxation and Productivity
    - Maintain a healthy balance between leisure and work activities.
    - Ensure that relaxation does not lead to neglecting responsibilities.

Integrating All Aspects in This Chapter

Combining proactive health checkups, letting go practices, maintaining mental health, and understanding personality types can create a holistic approach to well-being. Here's how to integrate these aspects into daily life:

1. Routine Health Checkups
    - Incorporate regular health screenings into your annual calendar.
    - Stay informed about personal health risks and preventive measures.

2. **Practice Letting Go**
   - Allocate time daily for mindfulness, meditation, or journaling.
   - Regularly assess and adjust your boundaries and commitments.

3. **Prioritize Mental Health**
   - Make mental health activities, like exercise, hobbies, social connections, a regular part of your routine.
   - Seek professional help when needed and do not hesitate to take breaks when overwhelmed.

4. **Understand and Adapt Personality Traits**
   - Recognize your personality type and adopt strategies to balance strengths and weaknesses.
   - Use the understanding of personality traits to improve interactions and relationships.

By proactively managing physical health through regular checkups, practicing letting go to reduce stress, prioritizing mental health, and understanding personality traits, we can achieve a balanced and fulfilling life. This holistic approach not only enhances personal well-being but also improves the ability to handle life's challenges effectively.

CHAPTER 8: LET GO

Conclusion: Turning Dreams into Destiny

Throughout this book, I have shared my journey from being a middle-class girl, the first in my family to go to college, and a non-native English speaker, to achieving remarkable milestones. I have become a vice president at a top financial firm, received numerous national and local awards, co-authored three books, co-purchased three homes, maintained a healthy 30-year marriage and given birth to three sons. As an entrepreneur, I have invested in the stock market and real estate, taken calculated risks, and dedicated countless hours to volunteering, all with the goal of making a difference in the lives of Hispanics living in the United States. Additionally, I have been nominated by the Governor of New Jersey and State of Florida representative to serve on commissions supporting minority groups.

I am an ordinary person who has applied the eight steps for success outlined in this book. Through tenacity and diligence, I have turned my dreams into reality. My personal anecdotes demonstrate practical ways you, too, can achieve your dreams.

Dare to Dream

Don't let your circumstances limit your aspirations. I grew up in a middle-class family and was the first to attend college. Dream beyond your limits and set your sights high.

Make a Plan

Chart your course with a clear and strategic plan. From buying homes to achieving professional success, every milestone began with a solid plan. Break down your goals into manageable steps and stay focused.

Stick to the Plan

Persistence pays off. Navigating challenges with determination helped me secure a vice president role and achieve other significant goals. Stay committed to your plan, even when faced with obstacles.

Be Grateful

Cultivating gratitude has been a powerful tool in my journey. It helps maintain a positive outlook and fosters resilience. Appreciate the progress you make, no matter how small.

Lift Others

The impact of lifting others on our journey cannot be overstated. Volunteering and supporting minority groups have been central to my mission. By helping others, you create a supportive community that propels everyone forward.

Feel Good

Embrace joy and cultivate positivity. Balancing career and family life, and finding joy in everyday moments, contribute to overall well-being. Make time for activities that make you feel good.

Find Your Tribe

Discovering your supportive network is crucial. Surround yourself with people who believe in your dreams. My family, friends, mentors, and colleagues have been instrumental in my success. Build and nurture your tribe.

Let Go

The liberating power of letting go is essential for renewal and growth. I learned to let go of control during challenging times, like my health battles and career transitions. Trust the process and be open to change.

Final Thoughts

By following these simple, methodic steps you, too, can transform your dreams into destiny. Each chapter in this book offers practical guides and inspirational stories to help you on your path. Whether you are in your twenties or sixties, these principles are timeless and universally applicable.

Reflect on your journey, recognize your achievements, and continue to dream big. The universe provides the tools, resources, and experiences you need at the right time. Trust the process, embrace challenges, and celebrate your successes.

Take the leap, apply these principles, grab the bull by the horns and turn your dreams into your destiny. You have the power to achieve greatness. Take action, your journey starts now!

FROM DREAMS TO DESTINY

About the Author

Claudia is a visionary of possibilities, a people connector, an international speaker, author, and award-winning champion for diversity and inclusion. As the founder of **elevink,** LLC, a social impact company, she is dedicated to increasing inclusivity and empowering underrepresented talent across America. She also provides coaching to new leaders and those seeking clarity in their career paths.

Claudia has shared her inspiring story and recipe for success at prestigious institutions including Princeton University, Wharton Business School, Rutgers, and Yale. With extensive national and local board experience, she is an active member of the Pasco County Commission on the Status of Women and serves as the Hispanic Star Tampa Hub lead. Her thought leadership is featured in notable publications, such as *Today's Inspired Latina Vol 5*, *Hispanic Stars Rising*, and *Today's Inspired Leader Vol 3*.

In recognition of her impactful work, Claudia has received numerous accolades. In 2020, she was honored with the Latina of Influence Award by Hispanic Lifestyle, the Red Shoe Movement Leader Award, and the Mujeres Brilliantes award from Prospanica. She was also named the Hispanics Inspiring Student Performance and Achievement (HISPA) Champion of the Year in 2018 and received the Young Hispanic Corporate Achiever award from the Hispanic Association on Corporate Responsibility (HACR) in 2007.

Claudia holds a B.A. in Psychology and an M.A. in Organizational Management. She is also certified in project management, Six Sigma Black Belt, and Agile professional methodologies, further underscoring her commitment to excellence and continuous learning.